THE PSYCHOLOGY OF RETIREMENT

SECOND EDITION

SUSAN MOORE AND DOREEN ROSENTHAL

W0114787

Routledge
Taylor & Francis Group

LONDON AND NEW YORK

Second edition published 2026
by Routledge
4 Park Square, Milton Park, Abingdon, Oxon, OX14 4RN

and by Routledge
605 Third Avenue, New York, NY 10158

Routledge is an imprint of the Taylor & Francis Group, an informa business

First edition published by Routledge 2019

British Library Cataloguing-in-Publication Data
A catalogue record for this book is available from the British Library

ISBN: 978-1-041-00813-2 (hbk)
ISBN: 978-1-041-00812-5 (pbk)
ISBN: 978-1-003-61178-3 (ebk)

DOI: 10.4324/9781003611783

Typeset in Joanna
by Apex CoVantage, LLC

https://routledgetextbooks.com/textbooks/thepsychologyofeverything/

THE PSYCHOLOGY OF RETIREMENT

How can you make the most of retirement? How should you plan for retirement? What are the challenges of retirement and how can they be dealt with?

This new edition of *The Psychology of Retirement* looks at this life stage as a journey that involves challenges, opportunities, setbacks, periods of disenchantment, and often, exciting new beginnings. Updates include a new chapter on the 'old age' stage of life as well as end-of-chapter tips and things to think about, case studies of retirees and pre-retirees, and new statistics including the effects of COVID and homeworking. Taking a positive approach, the book explores how retirement provides opportunities to cultivate new friendships, interests and hobbies, consolidate and renegotiate long-held ones, and even reinvent oneself in a post-work environment. It also emphasises the value of pre-retirement planning and the importance of establishing new goals and purposes.

Retirement can be a period of significant psychological growth and development, and *The Psychology of Retirement* shows how it can herald the beginning of a vibrant and active stage of life.

Emeritus Professor Susan Moore and Emeritus Professor Doreen Rosenthal are social researchers and retired academics who write extensively for both academic and non-academic audiences. They have jointly authored books on adolescence, sexuality, grandparenting, and retirement. They take their own advice about retirement, aiming to stay mentally, physically, and socially active.

THE PSYCHOLOGY OF EVERYTHING

People are fascinated by psychology, and what makes humans tick. Why do we think and behave the way we do? We've all met armchair psychologists claiming to have the answers, and people that ask if psychologists can tell what they're thinking. *The Psychology of Everything* is a series of books which debunk the popular myths and pseudo-science surrounding some of life's biggest questions.

The series explores the hidden psychological factors that drive us, from our subconscious desires and aversions, to our natural social instincts. Absorbing, informative, and always intriguing, each book is written by an expert in the field, examining how research-based knowledge compares with popular wisdom, and showing how psychology can truly enrich our understanding of modern life.

Applying a psychological lens to an array of topics and contemporary concerns – from sex, to fashion, to conspiracy theories – *The Psychology of Everything* will make you look at everything in a new way.

Titles in the series:

The Psychology of Artificial Intelligence
Tony J. Prescott

The Psychology of Trauma
Shanti Farrington and Alison Woodward

The Psychology of Menopause
Marie Percival

The Psychology of Fashion Second Edition
Carolyn Mair

The Psychology of the Extreme
Arie W. Kruglanski and Sophia Moskalenko

The Psychology of Stress
Charlotte Mottram, Alison Woodward, and Shanti Farrington

The Psychology of Sports Fans
Aaron CT Smith

The Psychology of Retirement Second Edition
Susan Moore and Doreen Rosenthal

For more information about this series, please visit:
www.routledgetextbooks.com/textbooks/thepsychologyofeverything/

CONTENTS

Acknowledgements   vii
Prologue   ix

1   What is retirement?   1

2   The journey: transitioning from worker to retiree   15

3   Financial security or financial stress?   33

4   Retirement, health, and wellbeing   49

5   Renegotiating social relationships   61

6   Reshaping identity in retirement   75

7   The next stage: old age   89

8   Making the most of retirement   99

Resources   111
Notes   115

ACKNOWLEDGEMENTS

We would like to thank our colleagues and institutions (the Centre for Women's Health, Gender and Society, Melbourne School of Population Health at The University of Melbourne, and the Department of Psychological Sciences at Swinburne University of Technology) for providing the resources that enabled us to complete the first edition of this book, as did research assistants Alex Poll and Kerrie Shandley. Special acknowledgement and thanks are due to the women and men who generously gave their time and considered thoughts as participants in our studies. Finally, our thanks once again to Ian and David, who sustain us always.

PROLOGUE

WHY A SECOND EDITION?

In 2015 we conducted large-scale studies of Australian retirees and grandparents. Both of us had been retired a couple of years; we were fit, active, and enjoyed travelling around to meet different retiree and seniors' groups and hearing their stories. The data we collected in survey, interview, and group discussion form helped shape and illustrate the first edition of *The Psychology of Retirement*.

Nearly ten years have passed! The world has changed, and so have we. We're older and not quite so fit and active, with some of the exciting options available when we first retired no longer feasible, for example, long-distance travel. Like so much of the rest of the world, we've had COVID, survived, and been motivated to think more deeply about vaccinations, infectious diseases, health care, and how epidemics are handled in aged care facilities and retirement villages. Sadly, the world is a less peaceful place with political turmoil in many countries. Cost of living increases have affected the financial stability of both older and younger generations, and this, paired with an ageing population and low birth rates, means that many must retire later than they might have chosen. We have attempted to capture the implications of these and other issues by updating the research presented in each of our original chapters, as well as adding a new chapter about preparation for the stage of life that some say begins around your 80th birthday – 'getting old'.

SO HOW HAS THE BOOK CHANGED . . .

In this second edition, as in the first, we follow the journey of today's retirees, through planning and decision-making, expectations, early experiences, pleasures, and disappointments. Factors influencing successful and unsuccessful coping with this life stage are considered, with particular emphasis on financial issues, health maintenance, social connectedness, and renegotiating identity in the retirement years. We describe the retirement experiences of both men and women, exploring similarities and differences in their resources and coping styles. We deal with questions of how successful retirement can be facilitated, and use current research to attempt to answer questions such as 'When is the best time to retire?', 'How can I plan for retirement?', and 'What are the pitfalls?'

One key issue in researching the retirement experience is that outcomes are readily conflated with the effects of ageing. If retired people show changes in their health status, for example, is this a function of their retirement, or is it because this group is experiencing ageing effects? A few careful studies have been able to separate out these effects (to some extent) either statistically or through comparing workers and retirees matched on age and other important variables like socio-economic status. There is a brief discussion of this issue in our chapter on health and retirement, but as well, we have added a chapter on the 'old age' stage of life. For those of us who are lucky enough to reach this stage, there are adjustments to be made and new goals to be set. Some of these goals might seem limited in relation to what can be achieved at age 60 or 70, but some are as important as any across one's lifetime, for example, decisions about leaving a legacy and finding meaning and comfort through life review.

The Psychology of Retirement draws on contemporary qualitative and quantitative psychological research, positioning this research within its social context. Throughout the book we draw on our own studies with seniors' groups (particularly a large-scale survey of retired Australian women), published works on grandmothers and grandfathers, and feedback from the men and women we have met during our many presentations to retiree groups. We quote liberally from these sources and our own experiences to illustrate and expand on findings from the social science literature.

1

WHAT IS RETIREMENT?

IS RETIREMENT REALLY 'THE NEW PROMOTION'?

What does it mean to be retired? How does it change your life? A dictionary definition of 'retire' is to 'leave one's job and cease to work, typically on reaching the normal age for leaving service'. That is certainly the traditional notion of this life transition. You have a pleasant morning tea with fellow workers, they present you with a gold watch or (more likely) a bunch of flowers, and off you go to your 'pensioned leisure', to play golf, do some fishing, or bake scones. The idea of retirement as 'the new promotion' certainly suggests this stage as one of well-earned leisure.

Shakespeare makes the 'promotion' sound rather less positive as he puts these words into the mouth of an ageing King Lear, describing his readiness to retire:

> And 'tis our fast intent
> To shake all cares and business from our age,
> Conferring them on younger strengths, while we
> Unburdened crawl towards death.

Simple, brutal, and, these days, inaccurate. Average life span in Shakespeare's time was somewhere between 30 and 40 years.

DOI: 10.4324/9781003611783-1

Those who were healthy and lucky enough to experience the luxury of retirement, were unlikely to live more than a few years longer. Even 100 years ago relatively few people lived to experience retirement, with life expectancy in the early 1920s being 55.6 for men and 59.6 for women.[1]

Compare these figures with modern times. According to the UK Office for National Statistics (2024) life expectancy at birth in Britain (between 2021 and 2022) was 78.6 years for men and 82.6 years for women.[2] It had increased by about eight years for men and six years for women since the early 1980s (and nearly 30 years since the 1920s). For those who avoid an early death and reach retirement age, lifespans are likely to be even longer. Using the same time frame, a 65-year-old man in the UK has, on average, a further 18.5 years of life remaining (bringing him to 83.3 years) and a woman 20.8 years (bringing her to nearly 86 years). Similar statistics characterise other English-speaking nations such as the US, Australia, Canada, and New Zealand, as well as many European countries. Our increased lifespans are accompanied by better health and fitness. Improvements in living conditions, diet and medical care, as well as greater public understanding of healthy lifestyles have contributed to this increase. It would be gloomy to spend these bonus post-retirement years doing little else but preparing for death. Post-retirement can extend to 10, 20, or 30 years, up to a third of our whole lifespan – longer than adolescence!

As the world population ages, retirees are becoming an increasingly large cohort. The baby boomer generation have reached their 60s and 70s. They are retiring en masse, drawing on their superannuation, government pensions and health care resources. Does this mean that retirees will become a drain on the economies of nations? Or will their capacity to contribute – for example, as consumers and investors, as carers of grandchildren and elderly relatives, as family mentors and supports – value add to society in ways that override the outcomes of non-participation in the paid workforce? Only time will tell, but it is clear that governments are worried about the economic effects of this large cohort, with many countries increasing the age at which social service and government pensions become available.[3] Of course, as seniors remain longer in paid employment, there will be a series of social effects, some intended, some unintended. These include effects on the labour market, on the 'volunteer workforce', and on the childcare, travel, and housing industries.

By way of balance, we should be aware that another feature of the expanding population of retirees is that this group forms a large voting bloc and so a voice to be listened to. Thus, there is pressure on governments to provide services for retired seniors, to hear our complaints and take note of suggestions. Retirees have power!

A NEW LIFE STAGE

Retirement offers us a new life stage with the chance for more experiences, more learning, more opportunities to set and achieve life goals, and further ways to contribute to our families, society, and our own development. Newly retired people are recognising this change, as we found through comments of participants in our research studies.[4,5] Many talked about new beginnings, rather than endings. Although all our informants self-defined as retired, some felt uncomfortable about the application of this word to the active ways they were engaging with life. They said things like:

> I see retirement as an opportunity to reinvent oneself.

> What is retirement? I have three volunteer workplaces, several elderly relatives and a grandchild to care for, a home and garden to keep, gym classes and more activities on offer than can be managed. What is quiet and retired about that?

> I didn't RETIRE, I simply stopped working in traditional sense. I did not stop working completely. The word 'RETIRE' here, implies that you leave one life for another.

Those researching retirement, like retirees themselves, can struggle with defining what it actually is. In an important review of the psychological literature, Wang and Shi (2004) point out how researchers have used many different definitions, including career cessation, reduced work effort, being in receipt of a pension or social security benefit, self-report, or having reached a certain age.[6] There are many ambiguities in these attempts. 'Career cessation', for example, can involve retiring from a long-term career and beginning another. People in our studies talked about retiring for a second or even a third time. As well, it can be difficult to pinpoint just when 'cessation' occurs if an individual moves from full-time to part-time to casual work modes.

Age is not a clear indicator of retirement status either. Some people never retire, particularly if they are self-employed. In most developed countries, a compulsory retiring age no longer exists except for a few specific occupations, usually those considered dangerous or requiring a high degree of mental or physical acuity, such as pilot, judge, or military personnel. The major constraints against retiring 'late' (say in your 70s or 80s) generally concern your health, your personal preferences, the availability of work, and your enjoyment of it.

Barriers against retiring 'early' (say, in your 50s) usually relate to personal preference and the availability of finances. Access to government pensions is rarely possible unless a specific age has been reached. In most Western countries, this entitlement age is between 60 and 65 years, but it is gradually rising as the world population ages and there are so many more retired people to be funded. Even drawing on your own retirement pension savings can attract economic penalties such as increased taxation if it occurs before a certain age.

Being on a government or superannuation pension does not necessarily indicate that you have retired, with many individuals working to supplement their pension incomes or simply for the pleasure of it. Some researchers have defined a retired person as one whose pension payments exceed the amount they earn in paid employment, but even a definition as seemingly objective as this does not necessarily align with people's self-reports.

Weiss (2005) suggested that retirement can be defined in three general ways. An *economic* definition relates to when an older person has ceased paid work; a *sociological* definition relates to when someone no longer works and has reached an age where this is socially acceptable; a *psychological* definition is when a person self-identifies as retired.[7] This book is directed at those who self-define as retired or preparing to retire, and although we discuss research that uses other definitions of retirement, it is a self-report approach that we prefer.

The slogan at the beginning of this chapter, presenting retirement as a kind of promotion, puts a new slant on this life stage, one that is very different from that encompassed in the King Lear quotation. Describing retirement as a 'promotion' reminds us of the potential for this stage to be positive, active and full of challenges, whichever way it is defined.

CASE STUDIES

Here are some individuals who have retired or are planning to do so.

Heather is 59 and really looking forward to getting away from office politics. In a year or two at the most, she hopes she'll have enough money to make a clean break from work and take time to relax and smell the roses.

At 65, Clara loves her job and doesn't really want to give it up just yet, but her husband has been retired for three years already and wants them to travel together before they're too old to enjoy it.

Martin was retrenched at age 63. He's received a good payout and his pension is adequate, but he feels 'consigned to the scrap heap' when he had so much more to give.

Lawrence enjoys his career and feels fit and healthy. He's decided to keep working past 70, provided he can negotiate part-time hours. This will give him freedom to do some planned home renovations (and play golf).

Sarina is giving up work as soon as her first grandchild is born so she can be a hands-on grandmother.

James was more than happy to retire on his 65th birthday. Now he's bored.

Do any of these people sound like you? In the next sections we consider the various reasons, types, and styles of retirement, and discuss whether our cases fit these models.

REASONS FOR RETIRING

Ideally, your retirement date will be chosen and planned for well ahead of time. Unfortunately, in the real world, such choice is not always possible, as in Martin's case. Workers in their 50s and 60s can be made redundant and find it difficult or even impossible to find other work. Some feel constrained to retire because of ill health, the needs of others, job stress, or problems dealing with changes in the workplace, such as the introduction of new technologies. Heather and Clara fit into this category.

Retirement wellbeing and ease of coping with this life stage are strongly related to reasons for retiring.[8] In our research, those made redundant were significantly less satisfied with their finances, their social life, their level of physical activity, their standard of living, and their life in general than those who left work voluntarily. They also rated themselves as significantly less financially secure than voluntary retirees, no doubt because they had a shorter length of time to plan for and accumulate savings and pension credits.

Research from all over the world indicates that, not surprisingly, men and women who are able to choose the time and circumstances of their retirement fare better in terms of retirement outcomes. Ill health, family pressures, and work organisational reasons for finishing work can all impact not only on finances but on future mental and physical wellbeing and quality of relationships. Of course, these are trends only. Many people 'bounce back' from a redundancy, find that life is less stressful in retirement, and/or are able, with greater rest and relaxation, to improve their health status post-work. Some examples from our research participants illustrate this kind of resilience.

> When I was made redundant, I decided to take it. I did not want to be deployed to another district or state. It was an enormously hard decision to make and be comfortable with. That sounds negative, but now I'm loving not having to work in such a stressful field of employment.

> I was very lucky that I was able to retire when I was made redundant, as I was then able to really support my parents in their last couple of years. My younger sisters were still very much working and could not take time to do this. They were very grateful I was managing it all. I was very glad I could do it.

RETIREMENT STYLES

There are at least three different styles of retirement.[9] First is the traditional 'cold turkey' approach, where paid work ceases altogether, as in the case of James in the previous section. One day you are a worker, next day a retiree with time to fill. Men and women who choose (or fall into) this approach do not necessarily fit the 'gone fishing' stereotype of spending their days in lazy leisure activities; many participate in volunteer work, care for grandchildren, involve themselves in clubs, play competitive sports, travel, garden, study, do home renovations – the list is endless. For this group there will be a likely fading of former occupational interests, links with past workplaces and identification as a 'worker'. Different self-definitions will emerge or strengthen, such as 'volunteer', 'grandparent', 'craftsperson', or 'golfer'. The risks for this group are loneliness, boredom, and social isolation. Without planning and organisation, time can hang heavy.

A second retirement style is the transitional approach, where people such as Lawrence gradually withdraw from the workforce through part-time or casual work. There may be no clear-cut moment when 'transitionals' define themselves as 'retired', so their identification as a worker remains for a longer time than for the 'cold turkey' retirees. Professionals, academics, and people running their own businesses often choose this form of gradual retirement where they ease out of paid work lives, taking time to try out and experiment with non-work interests and activities. One academic put it this way.

> I wound down over about five years, going from full-time to four days a week, then three days, then two. This way I was able to complete projects at work and hand over some of my responsibilities gradually. It also meant that over those five years I had a clear day each week to devote to my two pre-school grandchildren, but I also had excuses not to be too over committed to baby-sitting!

Such a model of gradual retirement has many advantages for those who enjoy their work but find that a full-time commitment becomes stressful as ageing proceeds and the recognition that life is finite becomes more powerful. A risk can be the difficulty of weaning yourself away from your worker identity and so delaying desired activities such as travel or relationship strengthening for too long. If you've always wanted to walk from Land's End to John O'Groats, probably better to try it at 60 than at 80. If you want to bond more strongly with your grandchildren, best not wait until they are teenagers or young adults.

The third retirement style has been labelled 'transformative'. Retirees in this group start on new projects (or even careers) that fill a good proportion of their day and provide a new identity, a new self-description. Sometimes these come about as a fulfilment of lifelong dream. An example would be the person who always wanted to express their creative side but had neither the time nor the financial flexibility to do so during their middle years. On retirement, this retiree takes art lessons, goes on painting tours, and sets up exhibitions. The former accountant or math teacher is now an artist. Sarina is another example. She sees her fulfilling new career as an active grandparent.

Transformative retirement may occur when individuals experiment and search for new ways to fill their time, and a particular interest or activity becomes a new passion. Sometimes it is simply serendipity – a chance meeting or an article in a newspaper set off a chain of events that culminate in a new career – paid or unpaid – for the retiree. Some examples:

> I didn't expect that a hobby I took up in retirement (decoupage) would provide me with the skill to set up my own little cottage industry. I worked hard at this, simply because I enjoyed it very much, and eventually made enough money at local craft markets to travel overseas for 2 two- and three-month holidays.

> I didn't expect my husband and I would start a charity. It has evolved far beyond our original vision and we are now engaged in succession planning.

One of the issues facing the transformative retiree is that they may find themselves needing to retire more than once! Indeed, these different ways of retiring are not mutually exclusive. A person might retire completely from their long-term career, spend a year or two engaged in leisure and domestic activities, then return to the same or a different workplace, either full time or part time. So long as a retiree's health is good and jobs are available, there is flexibility. In fact, writers now discuss the value of 'unretirement' as an excellent financial strategy, especially for those who took early retirement and find their funds dwindling more quickly than they expected.

RETIREMENT TYPES

Counselling psychologist Nancy Schlossberg developed a six-category retiree typology, focussing on psychological and behavioural characteristics rather than work patterns.[10] 'Continuers' maintained their pre-retirement interests and skills, using them in further work, volunteer, or hobby situations. The authors of this book have done just that, using our research skills post-retirement to write books on topics that we feel passionate about! 'Adventurers' began entirely new pursuits after retirement, often taking up activities they had little time for during their working years, such as travel or artistic endeavours. 'Searchers' experimented with a range of new activities, exploring many interests through trial and error. Less purposeful were the 'Easy Gliders', who enjoyed the freedom and flexibility of letting each day unfold but without any fixed goals, and the 'Retreaters', who disengaged from many former pursuits, wanting to wind down and reduce life stress. 'Involved Spectators' were also less active than Continuers, Adventurers, and Searchers, but while they shared some characteristics of Retreaters, they did maintain a high level of interest in the world around them. A retiree's type may be in part associated with personality characteristics, but as Schlossberg points out, it is also likely to be dependent on many other factors such as retirement age, mental and physical health, and financial and family circumstances. One's 'type' may also change as retirement (and age) progress; these should not be considered as fixed categories.

LOSS OF THE WORK ROLE

Why do lifespan psychologists consider retirement as an adjustment, a life change that requires a degree of coping and adaptation? Doesn't everyone want to give up work, relax, and do as they please? What's the problem here? Why all the fuss?

It seems that work – especially work you love – is fulfilling in more ways than just providing a pay packet. Of course we work to earn a living, but even jobs you don't particularly enjoy can have positive influences on your lifestyle. One famous study of unemployment, conducted in 1933 but still relevant today, delineated these 'latent' (or less obvious) functions of employment.[11] Marie Jahoda and her colleagues became participant observers of life in the Austrian village of Marienthal, where a key industry, employing most of the town, had recently closed. Most of the village were out of work. The resultant apathy, depression, and sense of hopelessness experienced by so many went beyond the deprivations associated with financial hardship.

In fact, this classic research study found that one of the major latent functions of work was that it helps us to structure our time. Although being unemployed and retired are not the same, they share the requirement that active steps are needed to restructure one's time once work no longer fills the days. Workers have a reason to get up at a certain hour each morning, a reason to stay groomed, fit, and alert. We have the reward of a limited amount of leisure time to look forward to when the workday is over. The unemployed can find they have too much free time; they feel bored and unmotivated without the structure that their employment once provided. When we asked retirees what they missed most about work, a significant number commented on this aspect.

> I miss the structure of a workplace where your work responsibilities and activities are clear.

> Perhaps the only thing [I miss] is that there was a structure to those days that I was working. Now I have had to ensure that my days are structured so that I do not bludge around.

Maintenance of social contact is another key latent function of work. There are people to chat with in most workplaces, although interestingly, the increasingly common phenomenon of 'working from home' may mean that home-based workers need to resolve issues of social isolation well before their retirement years. Nevertheless, in workplaces where one regularly meets fellow workers or customers, there is a social aspect to the day. Experiences and goals can be shared. Interactions with colleagues and workplace friends can be enriching, interesting, and broadening, giving the worker food for thought and conversational topics to share at home and with friends and family. There is no need to make special arrangements to set up workplace socialisation; it occurs as a natural part of the working day. One risk for retirees (and to some extent those who work from home) is social isolation and loneliness, unless a conscious effort is made to develop and maintain engagement with other people. We discuss this important consequence of retirement in a later chapter.

Retirees told us that social contact was one of the aspects of work they missed most, especially in early retirement before they had engaged with new social groups.

> I miss the companionship of working in a team. Miss some of the social connections that I once enjoyed.

> I initially missed being part of a 'team' but as time goes on, I have replaced my work team with many other social 'teams' and no longer miss the work team environment.

A third latent function of work is a sense of collective purpose (also alluded to in some of the previous quotes). Being part of a work team contributes to feelings of being useful and contributing to communal goals. These may be goals related to altruism (helping others), quality (making beautiful or functional items), production (improving last month's sales figures), service (satisfying customers), competition (becoming the most profitable division), or some other work values or combination of values. Retirees can re-establish such a sense of collective purpose in volunteer or creative work, or even in family projects, but to do so requires self-motivation and self-directedness that can be difficult to sustain. Retirees put it this way:

> I miss the clear purpose of each day and the plans and tasks that were laid out before me.

> [I miss] spending time each day working on projects that benefited the community and influenced how peopled lived. This provided a sense of having a broader purpose in life.

Another function of work – even the mere fact of being employed – is that it provides people with a certain status in life, an identity that is readily summed up in a few words – 'I'm a chemist' or 'I'm a car salesman'. This is particularly true of professional and skilled labour. The unemployed, and to some extent retirees, can feel stigmatised and that they are somehow of lower worth. One retired blogger, Syd, calls this 'the cocktail party dilemma'.[12] How do you answer the question about your working life that inevitably arises when you meet a new person? Syd discusses this and writes about her fear of being no longer interesting to others:

> After I retired, I found that telling people I was retired didn't have the same effect of propelling the conversation forward . . . Perhaps some people thought 'retired' was a euphemism for out of work . . . Other people responded by asking what I did all day, usually accompanied with the assertion that they would die of boredom if they retired. And to be fair, when you list out what you can recall that you actually 'do' all day, it does sound kind of boring.

Retired women we interviewed commented along the same lines.

> I miss the recognition and status.

> I miss the identity. Who am I without a business card?

Finally, jobs keep us active both mentally and physically. They keep us interacting with the world out there, exercising the mind and the body. The risk for retirees is in becoming unstimulated, unmotivated, and uninteresting. Certainly, retirement is an opportunity to take it easier, to enjoy rest and relaxation, but retirees also need interests and activities that excite, inspire, engage, and connect them with others. While some will retire with interests they cannot wait to pursue, others – especially the workaholic – will need time and effort to find new passions that provide both purpose and enjoyment.

One retiree summed up these work functions in her explanation of what she missed most about her working life.

> [I miss] the interaction with colleagues, a structure for the working week, the feeling that you are doing something worthwhile and interesting, learning new skills and maintaining existing skills, participating and cooperating with team and fellow workers on shared projects, belonging to something.

To summarise then, a major psychosocial challenge for retirees is to find new activities and ways of thinking to substitute for the functions that work once fulfilled in their lives. Throughout this book we discuss these in more detail as well as more and less successful approaches to making this transition.

QUESTIONS TO THINK ABOUT

Before you continue reading, it can be useful to consider your own feelings, motivations, and goals for retirement.

1. Do you agree with the idea that retirement is the 'new promotion', or does it feel more like a demotion to you?
2. What style of retiree are you (or will you be) – traditional ('cold turkey'), transitional (similar skills, fewer hours), or transformative (new career)? What do you consider to be the pros and cons of each?
3. What will (or did) you gain by retiring? What will (or did) you lose? [Consider your answer in terms of mental and physical health, finances, social status, relationships, activities, time management, goals, etc.]
4. Do you relate to any of the six case studies we have presented (Heather, Clara, Martin, Lawrence, Sarina, James)? Or are your retirement motivations quite different (or more complex)?
5. What are your retirement goals?

2

THE JOURNEY

TRANSITIONING FROM WORKER TO RETIREE

The process of retiring takes us on a psychological journey as we move from one life stage to another. The time it takes to make the physical transition to retirement – that is, to leave the workplace behind – will not necessarily correspond to the time it takes for the psychological journey. We are all different. Some who retire literally overnight will move seamlessly into planned activities, new roles, and greater involvement in already existing non-work roles such as grandparenting. Others will find themselves overwhelmed by the lack of structure in their lives and will take more time to adjust. For some, gradual retirement will assist adaptation to new roles; for others it might simply delay this process, stretching it out over a longer time frame.

Life transitions like retirement are developmental changes that involve discontinuities with previous life events. Discontinuities that occur quickly and are irreversible can be difficult to cope with, even when they are benign. Becoming a parent for the first time is an example of a sudden, irreversible life transition. While it may be wonderful and joyous, there will be ups and downs, heightened emotions and feelings of being overwhelmed. With time, new parents learn to adjust their lifestyles and expectations to create a new reality of 'family' instead of just 'couple'.

DOI: 10.4324/9781003611783-2

All transitions are like this, in that they require us to learn new ways of being and adjust to a different set of expectations and roles. When we retire, we move from a relatively predictable mode of existence into unknown territory. Do we still need to get up early and dress to impress? What tasks will we achieve, and who will we talk to today? What is there to talk about anyway, without the focus on workplace issues and our former colleagues? How will our workplace manage without us? These changes require emotional adjustment; they can be disorienting at best and depressing at worst. As well, our attitudes might need to change, especially if we have previously held negative stereotypes of retired people as 'past their use-by date'. Not the least of it, our sense of self will require cognitive restructuring. Who are we now, if not doctor, teacher, salesperson, administrator, taxi driver, business owner, or boss?

One writer, Cussen (2017), suggests there are six typical stages in the retirement transition.[1] These are planning (the pre-retirement phase), 'the big day' (farewells), the honeymoon period, disenchantment, reorientation, and re-establishing a routine. In this chapter, we expand on each of these in turn, keeping in mind that not all retirees will necessarily follow the same pathway or the same order of stages. It is possible that those who retire gradually over a period of years may work through their transition more gently. Not all retirees will experience a honeymoon period or a disenchantment phase. Those who retire for a second or even third time might have different experiences again. Forced redundancies and other pressures to retire are likely to make adjustment more difficult and its process lengthier than retirement occurring through free choice. Despite these caveats, many retirees will recognise their own experiences in Cussen's stages. Acknowledgement of their typicality may be a useful aid to self-understanding and provide guidance for those considering retirement in the future.

PLANNING

Imagining our own retirement is a precursor to planning for it. What were (or are) your thoughts about this life stage during your 20s, 30s, and 40s? Perhaps you conflated stereotypes of retirement with stereotypes of ageing, writing off these years as ones of disengagement and infirmity. Perhaps you envisaged an endless holiday, a time when you could finally sleep in, read or play golf all day, answering to no one. More likely you never gave retirement a second thought, except to sometimes notice the retirement fund deductions in your pay packet.

But as people reach their 50s and 60s, thoughts about retirement become more salient. It is not uncommon for workers to begin mental preparation for this change, through talking to others, seeking information, considering when to leave, developing appropriate exit strategies, examining finances, and thinking about activities and roles that might be part of a new post-work lifestyle. This is a healthy approach. Research is clear that planning assists adjustment and satisfaction with retirement. But it is not always easy to manage the headspace necessary for organising the future when the concerns of the present are pressing. For example, an Australian survey found around one-third of older workers (aged 55 or above) felt unprepared for retirement and had taken no action to prepare for it.[2]

Financial planning, which we discuss in detail in Chapter 3, is particularly important, but unfortunately many people find this difficult, boring, and anxiety arousing. One US study demonstrated that nearly half of a large sample of participants found it difficult to even think about, let alone plan, their retirement finances.[3] Very few of the workers surveyed had tried to calculate how much money they would need in retirement, or even understood how to go about doing this. Yet calculations of this sort are important in decisions about when might be the best time to retire. Delaying retirement even for a year or two can assist workers to pay off debts, increase savings, and sometimes gain more generous access to social security benefits and government pensions. In the US study, women especially felt overwhelmed, confused, and negative about financial planning, a task that many admitted to avoiding, even though they worried about it. Yet our studies and those of others show, not surprisingly, that those who make financial plans are more economically secure in retirement, a factor that is one of the strongest predictors of retirement adjustment and later life satisfaction. But planning is not all about money. As one retiree told us:

> Having had the experience, I think there is not enough mental preparation – I think it is like having a baby, you can read all about it, but until you experience it nothing you read makes sense.

Lifestyle planning – thinking about and arranging post-retirement activities, new roles and interests – is another important aspect of preparation for exit from the workforce. The move from structured time in the workforce to unstructured time in retirement can be a challenge. It may seem like a holiday at first, but after the first flush of freedom, time can hang heavy. Planning activities and setting some goals for the first few years of retirement are strategies likely to assist in alleviating the possibility of boredom or loss of purpose. You may need to experiment to find what you enjoy. What does seem important is to keep both mind and body active and to maintain social contacts, issues we discuss further in several chapters of this book.

Retirees from our study had plenty of comments and advice about lifestyle planning. The following three illustrate something of the variation in the extent to which plans are made – or not made!

> I planned my retirement with thought to ensure there were activities for Brain, Body and Soul.

> [If I had my time over] I'd devote more time to making a plan about what to do with all the extra time.

> [If I had my time over] I would have planned more activities. I got a bit of a shock when I first retired but quickly overcame lack of things to do. I found volunteering where I could use my brain and this is valued.

Of course, some people 'wing it' quite successfully, and others find their plans do not eventuate as circumstances change. Planning is a process, not a one-off activity. Flexibility is important as your world alters. Life events can turn plans on their head, as this retiree reminded us.

I am circumspect about perfect plans. Life is not like that.

SUCCESSION PLANNING

When you retire from a business or career, you might still have a stake in your company's future, for example in the welfare of staff or customers, in the financial health of the organisation, or in the maintenance of the legacy that you have left behind. The question arises as to who will take over your role. Is this something for which you have any responsibility or the capacity to influence? What will you leave behind? Who, if anyone, do you need to train? When should this process be implemented?

Succession planning isn't only for super-rich business families. It's something that business owners and managers, from mega-companies to small businesses, need to consider before they retire. Many employees, too, will have opportunities to have input in who succeeds them, and in orienting and training their successor.

The number of books written on this topic could fill a large library. If succession planning is a key issue for you, it is worth reading some of them or consulting an expert.[4,5] It is a process that takes time, thought, and communication. Discussions with others in your organisation are best begun well before your retirement date, especially if you are 'the boss' or hold an important position in the company. Issues to be considered include financial concerns, replacement skills needed, and the welfare of staff if the business is closing. For employees, sometimes it's as simple as having a coffee and a chat with your replacement or showing them around the building. Suffice to say, retirement will feel a more positive process if you can handle the handover with grace and good will.

FAREWELLING THE WORKPLACE

Whether your disengagement from the workplace comprises a one-off celebration or a long goodbye, a study by Van den Bogaard found that marking the event with some kind of public ritual is beneficial.[6] We celebrate other transitions such as 21st birthdays, weddings, and baptisms. These events are a social statement of the importance of the life change and the desire that it be recognised and accepted by colleagues, family, and friends. There is an implicit expectation that support will be available if needed for the individual facing their new life status. In the case of retirement, a send-off provides an opportunity for the retiring worker to both be acknowledged by and to acknowledge co-workers. It presents a clear message to all that one stage of life is over and a new one is beginning. A recent trend we have noted is for those about to retire to send thank-you emails to all who have mentored them and assisted in their career, as well as to current work colleagues. It's a positive way to assist maintaining current connections as well as re-establishing old ones.

HONEYMOON PHASE

The honeymoon phase is the recognition that so many of the constraints and stresses that surrounded you as a worker have now been removed. It's a realisation that is usually (but not always) accompanied by positive emotions like relief and joy. When we asked retirees to name the best aspects of their new life stage, 'freedom!' was so often the response. This was sometimes expressed as freedom to – 'to do what I want when I want', 'to no longer have a regimented lifestyle', 'to have control of my day-to-day activities', or 'to be able to do whatever I like for the first time in my life'. Others focused on their new-found freedoms from, especially from work-related stresses, as in 'no one to tell me what to do', 'no more conflicts with employees', 'not having to look after other people any more', 'not being subjected to bullying bosses', and 'not having to conform to a rigid schedule at work'.

Another benefit felt keenly by the newly retired is having more time. For many, this extra time meant simply 'sleeping in' or 'not having to rush off in the morning'; for others it was an opportunity to engage in new (or old) activities and interests or spend more time with family. Volunteering, studying, sports, fitness classes, and hobbies such as craft, reading, gardening, and travel were all mentioned as pursuits our retirees now felt they had time for.

The increase in time and freedom (or self-directedness) brought about by retirement does not stay a novelty forever. Some retirees tire of it after a short time. One female participant in a US study put it this way:

> At first it felt like a vacation for about three weeks and then it didn't feel so good anymore. I was just floundering around like a fish out of water. So I started to plan my day just like I did when I was at work. And that felt good! I felt like I had a purpose.[7]

For those who have organised (or fallen into) immediate post-retirement activities or projects such as extended travel or home renovations, the feeling that they now have *too much time* on their hands, and *too much freedom*, is likely to be delayed. For some, of course, that feeling never arrives, but many retirees do come to an awareness that, for their lives to be meaningful and self-fulfilling over the next decade or three, they need to develop new roles, new interests, and new ways to fill their days. Such awareness is sometimes preceded by the next stage in which the initial glow wears off and the realities of learning to cope with the changes of retirement hit home.

Longitudinal research from the European Health, Ageing and Retirement Study found evidence supporting the idea of a honeymoon period. A variable the researchers called 'agency-freedom', encompassing feelings of control, autonomy, self-realisation, and pleasure improved immediately post retirement (although a general measure of life satisfaction did not change). However, after two years of being retired, life satisfaction decreased – suggesting the beginning of a disenchantment phase.[8]

DISENCHANTMENT

> I must find something challenging to do! Crossword puzzles just don't cut it.[9]

> After longing for 'freedom' I got sick of that within 4 months. Is this all there is?

Cussen characterises this stage as the realisation that 'this is it', this is the rest of your life. It has the potential to be boring, to feel undirected and lacking in purpose. James, one of the cases we presented in Chapter 1, was keen to retire at 65 but quickly became bored, realising he missed work goals, the camaraderie and the structure of the working day. Retirees like James may experience apathy, lack of motivation, sadness, and even depression as they confront a future in which ageing is the only certainty. Disenchantment with retirement can occur more than once, as various projects or activities are completed and the retiree wonders what to do next. Some people have called it the 'retirement blues'.

It may be helpful for retirees to understand that the disenchantment phase is not uncommon – they are not alone or abnormal – it is part of the process of experiencing transition and change. As we age, these feelings may be particularly poignant as we recognise there is only so much time left, some of our life goals will never be fulfilled, and some of those we once had no longer seem important. Can we reframe our ambitions to make the most of each day left to us?

Relevant here is consideration of the work of developmental psychologist Erik Erikson, who wrote about how psychosocial maturity is something that grows and develops through different stages of life. At each life stage, he postulated a developmental 'crisis' to be worked through on the path to becoming a fully functioning adult. Resolution of each crisis may involve emotional upheavals and psychological costs. It's not only adolescents who experience existential angst, get moody and worry about what life has in store for them and how they will cope. Such feelings occur throughout life, particularly at periods of change.

For those at mid-life and beyond, Erikson emphasised the importance of developing a sense of generativity.[10] A generative person is one who makes contributions to society and future generations rather than focussing only on self-related concerns. Parenting is the usual – but not the only – path by which people make these contributions. Work too can contribute through one's productive efforts and through mentoring others. In Erikson's theory, the opposite of becoming generative is 'stagnation' – failure to find ways to contribute. Those who do not develop their sense of generativity feel disconnected from their community and from society in general; they may be self-absorbed, for example with the complaints of ageing or the need to appear young. The 'disenchantment' phase of retirement may be viewed as part of the struggle to move from this self-absorbed state to more mature fulfilment.

In retirement, some find generative fulfilment through grandchildren, but this path is not open to all. Retirement has the potential to lead to exacerbation of the generativity 'crisis' unless significant activities and goals can be substituted for those provided in the work environments. This reorientation of lifestyle is discussed next.

REORIENTATION: BUILDING A NEW IDENTITY

This is the stage where retirees ask questions like 'Who am I, now?' 'What is my purpose at this point?' and 'Am I still useful in some capacity?' Erikson might have phrased it as 'How can I justify my existence?' or 'How can I contribute?' Dealing with such issues can be difficult and is likely to involve experimentation, setbacks, and renegotiations. For example, expectations that you will spend significant time with grandchildren may not be realised, intentions to volunteer may be difficult to implement, or plans to travel may not come to fruition. You may face unexpected challenges like illness or death of a partner. However, experimentation with new and different activities, involvement with different kinds of organisations and meeting new people should be – and usually is – rewarding and fun. Over time, most retirees find new roles they enjoy, and new, satisfying ways to fill their days. Others do not achieve this resolution and find themselves discontented, playing out the role of grumpy old man or woman. In Chapter 6, we discuss in more detail the challenges of reshaping one's identity in the retirement years, particularly among those who have always been heavily committed to the workforce and find it difficult to let go.

ROUTINE: MOVING ON

Life changes, as we have seen, are often followed by disorientation, mood swings, experimentation, and setbacks. Eventually, we adapt to a new state of being. For some retirees, this adaptation comes swiftly and joyfully.

> It's better [than I expected]. I liked being a busy young thing and now I'm enjoying being a slow old thing.

> I am doing things I have meant to do for years! I organised a street party last January, such a hit and will repeat next summer! I have a VERY firm belief, retirement is what YOU make it, and I just LOVE having the freedom and choice each day. Love it.

For others, it can take longer and require adjustments to unforeseen circumstances. One felt she was 'marking time', while another jumped straight into a new activity:

> My retirement was earlier than I'd planned. My husband is still working for financial reasons so I sometimes feel I am marking time until we can do the travelling things together.

> I had been a workaholic and was surprised that I did not miss working very much at all. Overall, retirement is better than expected. However, I must admit that initially I replaced paid work with a heavy dose of volunteer work, which I have now eased back on, and have finally, 10 years after retirement, achieved a better work/life balance for the first time in my life!

Over time, most retirees develop a new, non-work identity. New routines, different social worlds and reimagined goals are established. Many describe these years as the best of their lives. One factor affecting successful adaptation to retirement is choosing the 'best' time to go. In the next section, we consider a range of variables that influence this decision.

WHEN IS THE BEST TIME TO RETIRE?[11]

WHEN YOU CHOOSE

The best time to go depends on many different factors, but as we saw in Chapter 1, one of the strongest predictors of retirement satisfaction is being able to make that choice on your own terms. An unexpected redundancy, as well as reducing your opportunity to make adequate financial and lifestyle plans for retirement, can be experienced as a blow to self-esteem, a dismissing of your past contributions to the workplace. Similarly, retiring because of job stress can feel like personal failure. Even when a difficult workplace is left behind, residual trauma is a possibility that can lead to periods of anxiety and depression. Negative emotions such as these can have flow-on effects, putting strain on your spouse, family, and friendships and exacerbating the situation further. Such setbacks may be partially ameliorated by factors like a generous redundancy payout (if you are lucky enough to receive one!), a supportive family and social group, interests and goals you wish to pursue outside of the workplace, good health, and personal resilience.

If retirement feels premature or pressured, one strategy for coping is to seek other work, even if it is not at the pay rate, status level, or time fraction to which you have been accustomed. A bridging period of part-time or casual employment, if available, can aid the transition to retirement by allowing more time for planning and 'getting used to' the idea. It is also helpful to be able to talk through your disappointments and develop new life plans with someone who is detached and non-judgemental, such as a counsellor.

WHEN YOU'VE GOT ENOUGH MONEY

As we mention on many occasions throughout this book, it will be much more satisfying if you can retire with adequate savings and pension entitlements to meet your lifestyle requirements.

How much do you need? This is not an easy question to answer. But before you make a decision to retire based on finances, it is important to gain a sense of the income you will need to maintain a comfortable lifestyle. What exactly are your entitlements? Do you have a sense of your day-to-day expenses and how are they likely to change in retirement? How long do you expect to live? Do you have any debts or any major expenses coming up? Have you made plans for post-retirement travel, house renovations, or other big spends? Would you be prepared financially if faced with a significant but unexpected expense, such as a health crisis? Other important questions to ask yourself include whether there are part-time or casual jobs available if you need to top up your savings, and whether your current investments are performing adequately. The general state of the economy can have a marked effect on retirement plans, as evidenced by the Global Financial Crisis of 2008 that saw many people delay their retirement to earn back some of the funds they had lost when the stock market fell.

Similarly, the COVID pandemic of 2020/21 and accompanying lockdowns played havoc with the work opportunities and retirement savings of many, especially those employed in certain industries such as small businesses, hospitality, tourism, and entertainment. Some recent research argues that the 'traditional' retirement age of around 65 years is becoming less and less feasible due to 'cost of living crises' around the world. Indeed, the OECD predicts that the average retirement age will have increased by two years by the 2060s, partly due to financial constraints and partly due to increased lifespan.[12]

A sensible plan is to seek advice from a financial counsellor or trusted economic advisor if you are not sure about your financial status. If you believe your finances are inadequate, consider the pros and cons of working another year or two, perhaps in a different job. Interestingly, it is not uncommon for people to work well beyond their need to economically support a comfortable retirement because they enjoy their job and feel healthy and motivated to continue longer. Everybody is different.

WHEN YOUR HEALTH TELLS YOU

It's not only poor health that can lead to a decision to retire. Sometimes it is good health. One thing people do as they enter their senior years is speculate on how much time they have left. In relation to the things you want to experience and achieve in life – your bucket list – this can be a mind-focussing exercise. Many are motivated to retire while still in good health, 'before it is too late'. Retirees we talked to gave advice like 'travel early in your retirement, while you still have your health' and 'don't wait too long to do the things you really want to do'.

Retiring because your physical or mental health is poor is, of course, far less satisfying, a conclusion backed up by ample research. While retirement allows greater opportunities to rest, relax, and respond to treatment, the transition in itself can be stressful – as we have seen – with the potential to exacerbate negative mood, especially if you are socially isolated. Can you take some sick leave instead, ask to be assigned to lighter duties, or work part-time? For some, these options may allow heath to be maintained or chronic illness symptoms stabilised. Retirement can be worked toward more gradually and social supports put in place to assist not only with health care but also with making the change from worker to retiree.

On the other hand, Sohier and colleagues in their large-scale European study found that retirement can be a relief for those older workers in 'poor quality' jobs, that is, in occupations for which the physical and/or mental stresses outweigh rewards. For this group, wellbeing was likely to improve post-retirement.[13]

WHEN YOU'RE READY TO DISENGAGE FROM YOUR JOB

Being in a job you love can be a great buzz. People who are lucky enough to work at what they enjoy are more likely to delay retirement. Higher levels of education are associated with delayed retirement, perhaps because the well-educated are more likely to be in occupations that are interesting, fulfilling, and associated with better working conditions. Those who live for their work, are 'workaholics', and/or cannot imagine life without the challenges of their occupation will tend to put off retirement and may find the transition a difficult one, a topic we discuss in more detail in Chapter 6 on reshaping identity.

WHEN THE STARS OF FAMILY LIFE ARE IN ALIGNMENT

Women are far more likely than men to cite family reasons for retiring. Studies indicate that married women tend to coordinate their retirement date with their partner's retirement intentions often so they can retire together.[14] Couples are more likely to time their retirements to coincide if they enjoy each other's company.[15] A significant proportion of retired women we surveyed said they retired for family reasons, including the desire to spend time with their partner, travel together, and share activities. Some commented on how successful this had been; others were disappointed that their husbands 'did not want to get off the couch' or that their relationship was not standing up well to both being home all day. Sadly, the plans of some women had to be adapted or abandoned when their partners fell ill or died early in the retirement years.

Another key family reason for retirement is to care for grandchildren. A large-scale longitudinal study in the US showed that the arrival of a new grandchild increased the probability of a woman retiring by 8 per cent.[16] We have spoken to many grandmothers who either retired or moved to part-time work in order to assist with grandchildren and bond with them in their pre-school years.

In comparison to retiring to have fun with a loved spouse or enjoy your grandchildren's childhoods, retirement for some family reasons can be extremely stressful. Examples include the need to leave the workforce to take on full-time caring responsibilities for an elderly relative, a disabled spouse or grandchildren whose parents cannot cope. Sarina, one of our cases, plans to retire as soon as her first grandchild is born, but it is important that she discuss these plans in advance with the grandchild's parents. They may have very different ideas about the type and amount of childcare they require, ideas that may not be compatible with Sarina's expectations.

Even if leaving the paid workforce to spend more time with family is for the happiest of reasons, there can be relationship stresses. Household roles and responsibilities may need renegotiating. Expect a period of adjustment. If family pressures to retire present difficult and challenging circumstances, adjustment will take longer, and your coping resources will be stretched. It is important to consider all your options, seek the support of others, and not become a martyr to your caring responsibilities, an issue discussed further in Chapter 5 (Renegotiating social relationships).

WHEN THERE ARE OTHER THINGS YOU WANT TO DO BESIDES WORK

You've always wanted to study archaeology, set up a local catering business, learn Italian, write your family history, play more golf, go deep sea fishing, or travel to far-flung places. Retirement can be your time. As one of our study participants said, 'Full-time work became too demanding with all my other commitments and hobbies!' One of the most satisfying reasons to retire is to take up interests and activities that you are passionate about. Even when goals don't quite come to fruition – like trying to learn the piano at age 65 (possible but very difficult) – you can have fun trying.

So there is no ideal age to retire that will suit everyone. It's best though if you can choose your own time, when you are ready to leave behind or modify your workplace identity and seek other challenges. It's best if you are not pressured to leave by work, family, or health concerns, and when your finances and social networks allow you to maintain a comfortable, connected lifestyle and indulge in interests and activities you enjoy. Of course, life does not always follow this idealised course. Luckily, we humans are an adaptable species. It is also worth noting that retirement decisions need not be irreversible for everybody. Bridge employment, casual work, or even new careers are desirable and achievable options for many retirees.

MORE THINGS TO THINK ABOUT

When should you start planning for retirement? Some say it can't be too early!

Here are some suggestions depending on your age. We follow up many of the points made here in subsequent chapters.

Under 30s. These will be the ages when you are learning about the world, getting on with formal education, planning and beginning your career, hopefully enjoying your youth. Too early to worry about retirement perhaps? On the other hand, it doesn't hurt to begin learning about financial matters, saving, investing, and the types of insurance and pension plans that might be suitable for your age group. Different countries have different systems in place to enable you to save for retirement. Do you know if the nation in which you work has a compulsory savings plan for retirement? Or a welfare scheme for the aged non-employed?

Aged 30–49 years. Hopefully, you are getting established in your career path but you're also likely to have many commitments such as family expenses and either rent payments or a mortgage on your home. Can you spare any money to save for retirement? It's difficult but important to have a trustworthy, credible pension savings plan in place, even if the amounts you are putting aside seem small (they will grow if the plan invests wisely). Have you thought about what age you'd like to retire and how much you'll need to live on? Are you looking after your health and stress levels to give yourself the best chance for a happy, heathy retirement? Despite everything on your plate at the moment, are you managing to maintain strong family relationships and friendships? So much to think about!

Aged 50 to early 60s. Now you really must begin to think about retirement! How much more do you need in your savings, and how will you get it? Have you revised your planned date of retirement? On what basis? What goals have you begun to set for when the day arrives? Are you hoping to maintain some part-time work in your current field or a different area? Do you have more plans than 'have a rest and spend the kids' inheritance'? Do your plans sound like those New Year Resolutions that last about a week? If you've decided to 'lose weight, get fit, and give up alcohol', how will you sustain these goals longer than you've previously managed?

Mid 60s to 75 years. You've already retired or thinking seriously about it. If retired, what's working for you and what isn't? What can you do next to turn around the negatives? Would part-time work assist your financial position, and is it feasible for you? Have you talked to a financial planner? Have you considered taking some courses, volunteering, or joining a seniors' group? Are mental and physical exercises built into your day? Health checks are especially important for this age group; don't neglect them. Still got some things left to do on your bucket list? Better do them sooner rather than wait too long!

Over 75s. As we reach older ages, it can be therapeutic to reflect on your life, remember the high points and process the lows if you can. Maybe you won't be able to fit so much into your day, but you can still have fun! Treasure your family and those who emotionally support you. If you're still working, well done! If you're not, that's fine too.

3

FINANCIAL SECURITY OR FINANCIAL STRESS?

Retirement is expensive; the bills come in but not the income.[1]

Financial security is one of the most important single issues for retirees. When asked the 'worst thing' about retirement, one quarter of our study participants nominated worries about money. Research in several countries suggests that a high percentage of workers are continuing to work beyond pension eligibility age because of concerns about money. As one writer commented, 'Retiring in your 60s is becoming an impossible goal'.[2] Whether retirees have adequate financial resources for their retirement is of critical concern not only to retirees themselves but also to the community at large, given the cost implications of financial poverty among a relatively large (and increasing) sector of the population.

Retirement can become a time of poverty with a significant number of people finding themselves in financial and psychological stress as their retirement years add up. Indeed, many retirees enter this period of their life without the necessary savings or entitlements to support them as they age.

Traditionally retirement financial resources have derived from three 'pillars': personal superannuation by employers and employees

DOI: 10.4324/9781003611783-3

while working, government pensions, and savings. Superannuation is designed to ensure funds are available for a comfortable retirement, but the balance available on retirement suggests this is unlikely, especially for women whose funds, on average, are significantly less than those of men. For example, the Association of Superannuation Funds of Australia notes that Australian women on average have 25 per cent lower super balances than men when they retire.[3] Low wealth, little or no retirement savings, and longer life expectancy result in many individuals having to rely on government pensions and/or welfare-based schemes as their main or only source of retirement income. And even in wealthy Western countries, pensions are often barely adequate to sustain even a modest post-retirement lifestyle.[4]

As an example, in 2022, a survey of consumer finances by the US Federal Reserve Bank showed that almost half of American households had no savings in retirement accounts. Even among older cohorts, many Americans are not prepared for retirement, with total savings falling well short of what is needed for adequate living once paid work ceases.[5]

It's just as bad for retirees in the UK where a report[6] showed one in seven people due to retire in 2017 admitted to having no workplace or personal retirement savings and 11 per cent of those expected to be totally or somewhat reliant on the state pension in old age. Not surprisingly financial stress in retirement was reported by more than one in three, who said they were struggling to make ends meet. The situation had not improved by 2021, when British census data showed that between 2018 and 2020, one-third of people did not expect to have any pension provision beyond the state pension when they retired.[7] A worker retiring and relying solely on the flat-rate State Pension would have an income falling short of estimates of the minimum standards by a substantial amount, an effect exacerbated in times of high inflation. Those with lower retirement savings were over-represented among the self-employed, people with long-standing illnesses or disabilities, and those from minority ethnic groups.

Even for those who have saved carefully for their retirement, other factors may reduce their nest egg. Taxation results in loss of savings income; savings are not protected from inflation unless wisely invested (which requires effort and knowledge); savings may have been sufficient when people did not live as long but need to be much higher to provide an income stream for 20–30 years post-retirement. As well, with increased housing prices leading to first home buyers generally being older than they once were, mortgage and other debts are more likely to carry over to the retirement years and reduce funds for day-to-day living.

THE GENDER GAP

I would never have handed over all my wages to my husband, nor co-signed loans for his business, or become guarantor for anyone. I regret being financially disabled all my married life of 47 years. Life has taken a definite downturn since I retired – I live from pension to pension.

The gender gap in wages is a key driver in women's poorer resources on retirement. Most retirement income systems do not take account of the different work patterns of women and men and structurally favour those who work full time without breaks for their entire work life. If you do not fit this pattern, you are significantly handicapped when saving for your retirement.

There are several interrelated work, family, and societal factors that influence the pay gap. Women typically occupy lower paid roles in the workforce and lower paid occupations than men; they are more likely than men to work part-time or casually; and they are more likely to take breaks in their employment for childrearing or to provide unpaid care for others. Largely because of these responsibilities, women have a more precarious attachment to the workforce, often working in casual jobs. Additionally, although the situation is improving over time, job discrimination, both direct and indirect, still exists.

A commonly cited example of this phenomenon is the gender difference in Chairs and/or Chief Executive Officers of major public companies. One might suggest that women are seriously disadvantaged by this, given the importance of these roles for company equity policies, including an understanding of women's particular work patterns, and their potential influence of these individuals on government policy.

In all countries where senior executives' salaries are examined, women are hardly represented. In the US, the Standard & Poor's 500 index (S&P 500) is an index of 500 stocks seen as a leading indicator of equities. Women held only 29 (5.8 per cent) CEO positions in these companies when we wrote the first edition of this book.[8] In 2024, the number had increased marginally to 31.[9] In Australia in 2024, women remained under-represented in the most senior corporate positions within the top 300 companies listed on the Australian stock exchange. Only 8 per cent of women (25) were CEOs, and 82 per cent of individuals in the 'CEO pipeline' (that is, in training for CEO positions) were men.[10]

Looking more broadly at the gender differential in pay, a recent OECD report showed in 2022 the difference between women's and men's median wage varied dramatically from 1.1 per cent in Belgium (down from 3.3 per cent in 2014) to 31.2 per cent in South Korea (down from 36.7 per cent in 2014). Most Western countries including the UK, US and Canada, Australia and France had gaps of between 10 and 14 per cent. Although the gaps had lessened since 2014, in no country did women earn more than men.[11]

The situation is worse if we turn to the lifetime accumulation of assets (the gender wealth gap). Not unexpectedly women fare badly relative to men. Women not only have less total wealth than men, they also have fewer diverse assets and are more likely than men to have their assets in a family home; in fact, the family home has become the key form of wealth for many women. Another factor contributing to the gender wealth gap is women's earlier retirement from the workforce compared to men. Early retirement is likely to lead to drawing down of financial resources, while retiring later has clear economic benefits, including earned wages, and possibly employer-provided health insurance and retirement plan contributions. These financial benefits accrue rapidly; for example, we know that working two more years has a significant impact on the preservation of retirement wealth for American workers.

FINANCIAL PLANNING

I am a grasshopper. I lived from pay to pay. I did not save or plan.

I applied the ideals about being financially savvy. I was most of my life, because I attended a very good seminar when I was very young, so I got my financial savviness from that.

Would it surprise you to know that our first quote is from a woman and the second from a man? Without wishing to reinforce stereotypes, these quotes encapsulate the differences between many women and men in their financial planning for retirement. Numerous studies find that women's planning for retirement has not matched their concerns about the need for financial security. In several studies, nearly double the number of men compared with women claimed they were mostly responsible for financial and retirement planning in their households.

Probably even more important than gender in making effective financial plans is the general economic climate. According to a 16-country study comprising over 18,000 participants, a major predictor of whether economic wellbeing in retirement is considered a key financial concern is workers' success in putting some of their income aside in the previous 12 months.[12] More immediate financial challenges (such as feeding one's family or making rent/mortgage payments) were of greater concern than retirement saving, particularly for women, individuals over 40 years, those with lower levels of education, and most strongly and not surprisingly, those with lower incomes. As the study authors suggest, while the accumulated effects of population ageing and low economic growth increase the need for workers to make economic plans for retirement, the problems of doing so are accentuated in difficult economic times.

Even those who have adequate income to make effective financial arrangements for retirement are not always able to do so. A nationwide

US study showed that most retirees, and more women than men, wanted help from a professional in managing their investments, especially for specific aspects of retirement planning such as budgeting.[13] There was also considerable demand for help with their overall financial 'health'. Why the lack of planning and the need for outside help? Financial literacy and risk management are two important factors that affect investment decisions and successes.

FINANCIAL LITERACY

The most common measure of financial literacy, and one that is used in most if not all research on this topic, consists of five questions about interest, inflation and risk diversification, housing prices, and long-term investment.[14] Although a limited measure, the questions do cover concepts most relevant to savings and investment decisions.

1. Risk: Do you think the following statement is true or false? 'Buying a single company's stock/shares usually provides a safer return than a stock mutual fund/managed investment fund'. Answers: 1. True, 2. False, 3. Don't know. Correct answer: False.
2. Interest: Suppose you had $100 in a savings account and the interest rate was 2% per year. After 5 years, how much do you think you would have in the account if you left the money to grow? Answers: 1. More than $102, 2. Exactly $102, 3. Less than $102, 4. Don't know. Correct answer: More than $102.
3. Inflation: Imagine that the interest rate on your savings account was 1% per year and inflation was 2% per year. After one year, how much would you be able to buy with the money in this account? Answers: 1. More than today, 2. Exactly the same, 3. Less than today, 4. Don't know. Correct answer: Less than today.
4. Housing prices: Do you think the following statement is true or false? 'Housing prices in [your country] can never go down'. Answers: 1. True, 2. False, 3. Don't know. Correct answer: False.
5. Long-term investment: Considering a long time period (for example 10 or 20 years), which asset described here normally

gives the highest returns? Answers: 1. Stocks/shares, 2. Bonds, 3. Savings accounts, 4. Precious metals, 5. Don't know. Correct answer: Stocks/shares.

How did you score? Worldwide data suggest that levels of financial literacy are low across most countries. For example, a report by the Global Financial Literary Excellence Center covering many countries found on average only one-third of adults demonstrated 'adequate' financial literacy, with lower rates for women than men.[15] A comprehensive literature review of research in this area[16] confirmed 'severe' levels of financial illiteracy among women, especially among single women and widows. There are also significant differences according to income levels and racial/ethnic groups. A US study of almost 10,000 adults (mean age 54 years) showed the average score to be approximately three out of five questions correct. Scores for Blacks and Hispanics were on average significantly below those of Whites at each income level, although differences between racial/ethnic groups decreased as income increased.[17] Reasons for these differences could relate to factors such as discrimination, opportunity, education, and interests, as well as cultural and gender norms or stereotypes.

Why is it important to be financially literate? There is considerable agreement that financial literacy has a positive impact on financial behaviour and financial status. Financially literate individuals do better at a range of financial behaviours, including budgeting, saving money, and planning for retirement. The link between literacy and important financial decisions means that women, low-income individuals, and certain minority groups are particularly disadvantaged when it comes to planning for retirement and accumulating retirement wealth.

FINANCIAL RISK

A second key driver in increasing retirement wealth is the extent to which people are willing to make financially risky decisions. Conservative decisions are those that involve taking few risks with your savings and investments, for example putting money into low-interest but safe bank accounts or only buying blue chip stocks and shares. Such cautious behaviour is likely to be relatively safe but often means that the growth of your retirement nest egg will not keep up with inflation. While most people recognise how high inflation rates make saving difficult (because the cost-of-living increases), fewer are aware of the extent that savings can rapidly lose their value/buying power. If your retirement savings increase by 2 per cent per year, but the cost of food and housing goes up by 5 per cent over the same period, you will be worse off financially. On the other hand, high-risk investment strategies are ones that can make or break you. These are strategies to be used sparingly unless you have deep pockets and/or have done your research thoroughly.

Moderate financial risk taking is advised by financial experts as the most effective investment strategy in the longer term. This generally involves diversifying assets so that risk is spread over a range of different options, at a range of different risk levels – not putting all your eggs in the one basket. One hopes these strategies will allow investments to keep up with inflation while remaining relatively safe.

Financial risk aversion refers to over-reliance on low-risk invest-ment strategies. While sensible in the short term, across the longer term of saving for retirement, being financially risk-averse will usually result in lower asset levels for the retiree. Financial risk has been the subject of many past research studies with the extremely robust result that women are more risk-averse than men. Coupled with poor finan-cial literacy, risk-averse attitudes to financial investment over their work life may leave women at a disadvantage compared to men, and often without the ability or willingness to make the best possible financial decisions before or during retirement.

Why are women more risk-averse than men? One explanation relates to gender inequalities in wealth and the different roles that impact on these inequalities, including gender discrimination in labour and credit markets, investment advice and information on investment decision-making. If your income is low, there is a lot to be lost by taking financial risks, and on balance, it may seem as though there is little to be gained.

Perhaps the last word should be left to one of our anonymous survey respondents. Asked what they would do differently, many women wrote at length and in negative terms about financial issues.

> I would try not to have breaks from paid employment, so that I would have been able to contribute more to superannuation. I would have been able to contribute longer to super (super did not exist when I first started working). I would have found out more about financial investment prior to retirement. I would have tried to have funds available to start investing in the property market sooner (for most of my early working life I lived pay to pay as I was a single mother with one wage).

Given that financial planning has clear benefits for a comfortable retirement, the task for policymakers is to encourage and support individuals to plan wisely well in advance of leaving the paid workforce.

A KEY CONSEQUENCE OF FINANCIAL STRESS

> I expect to be poor; I may become functionally homeless.

Financial stress can have many negative consequences for retirees, requiring or leading to significant changes in lifestyle. Of these, the need to leave one's home is a major outcome. At least one study has shown late mid-life workers and retirees expect to remain at home as they age, but for retirees living in circumstances of financial stress, this is often not an option. It's costly to maintain a family home, and this can be beyond the limited financial resources of some retirees. While the need to seek other housing may be due to factors other than financial stress (such as poor health, serious chronic illness, or death of a partner), loss of income on retirement is a major reason for seeking lower-cost accommodation. The need for this is especially acute for single female retirees who do not (and did not) have the earnings of a partner to help with finances. As one woman said, 'I was paying about 70 per cent of my income, which was a pension, on rent'. Even those with a small nest egg find they have to access this if they are on a pension in order to survive in an increasingly expensive private rental market.

> I previously rent[ed] on my own but due to the rent going up I couldn't keep up with it and have had to move in with my friend who has Parkinson's [disease] and is not a stimulating or interesting person to be around. I've been forced to do this in order to save some money, but I can assure you that it is certainly not from choice.

For retirees who are renters, there is a potential loss of security of tenure as well as difficulties in finding suitable accommodation at an affordable cost, as the previous quote indicates.

What options do retirees have if they cannot remain in their pre-retirement home? Retirement villages are a common choice, although there have been serious concerns raised about the financial costs of these, as well as 'terms and conditions' that are not always well understood on entry and can be detrimental to maintaining quality of life. Other options available include downsizing to a smaller alternative or to move to a cheaper location. Although either may result in a better financial situation, they can also involve less positive outcomes such as losing a cohort of neighbourhood friends and having to develop a new social network. Moving in with children (and grandchildren) is another solution to financial problems, but this can be fraught with disagreement. Multigenerational living can save money, but disputes around finance are common if sharing of expenses is perceived to be unreasonable. Retirees may find it hard to give up their independence and chafe at having to abide by family rules. This problem can be overcome if there is a place where each person has some area which is private, like the 'granny flat' of old that allowed for separate living with the security of having family nearby and with significant cost savings. Whatever the option taken, there are costs as well as benefits in leaving one's family home after retirement. And for some retirees with very little in the way of financial resources, homelessness may be the ultimate end result.

BEWARE SCAMS AND FRAUDS

A scam happens when somebody gains your confidence through trickery in order to steal your money or information. Account fraud takes place when your bank or investment funds are accessed without your knowledge or authority, for example, through hacking institutional records. In the 12 months between 2022 and 2023, 8.7 per cent of Australians (1.8 million) experienced credit card fraud and 2.5 per cent experienced a scam. An additional 3.1 per cent experienced identity theft or theft through targeting by online impersonators.[18] One example is the 'hi mum' or 'hi grandma' scam in which a scammer impersonating a relative sends a text asking for money urgently, for reasons such as having their wallet stolen and needing to pay for goods or even being held for ransom.

Unfamiliarity with the less visible aspects of browsing the web (firewalls and built-in virus protection, for example) and lower levels of digital literacy in general make seniors especially susceptible to scams. It is quite common for scammers to send email messages that appear to be from a legitimate company or institution, asking them to 'update' or 'verify' their personal information. A 2023 survey among internet users in the United Kingdom (UK) found that 90 per cent of the users between 16 and 24 years were confident that they could identify scam e-mails, compared to only 65 per cent of those aged 65 years and older.[19]

Those of retirement age are also vulnerable to investment scams as they search for ways to manage their post-retirement pension and investment income. Such scams involve convincing the individual to part with money on the promise of a questionable financial opportunity. From pyramid schemes to complex financial products that many economists don't even understand, investment schemes have long been a successful way to take advantage of older people.

Door-to-door and home maintenance scams are a further example of financial exploitation. While many legitimate businesses sell things door-to-door, scammers also use this approach. These types of scams generally involve promoting goods and services that are of poor quality or not delivered at all. Unscrupulous contractors convince victims they are in dire need of various home repairs. Then they overcharge them or take money before the projects are completed and then disappear.

IF YOU SUSPECT YOU'VE BEEN THE VICTIM OF A SCAM . . .

Tell someone you trust; don't be afraid or embarrassed. Others have had similar experiences, and there are people and organisations that can help. If you do nothing, you may be exposed to another scam, and at the least, you give scammers the opportunity to prey on others. Keep handy the phone numbers and resources you can turn to, including the local police and your bank. The best protection against scams is to know how scammers operate. Don't be pressured into making a decision; be suspicious of requests for money even if they seem official; verify the identity of the contact, for example, by calling the relevant organisation directly; ignore phone calls or emails offering financial advice or opportunities; be suspicious of unexpected emails or letters advising you how to claim an inheritance or competition prize; regularly change your passwords; and importantly, be aware of and understand your consumer rights.

ELDER FINANCIAL ABUSE

Sometimes thought of as a scam, elder financial abuse is not carried out by strangers, but by someone known and trusted by the older person, usually a family member. Financial abuse is an increasing phenomenon in Western nations, as both lifespan and the cost of housing increase. Some have called this phenomenon 'inheritance impatience'. Adult children can become frustrated at being unable to afford housing or other aspects of lifestyle while perceiving their parents to be 'sitting on resources' such as the family home, 'wasting' their inheritance on retirement leisure activities, distributing their finances unequally among their children, or even threatening to leave their money to charity. More likely to be the victims of elder financial abuse are seniors who live alone, are socially isolated, have cognitive deficits, and/or who rely on a family member for care. In worst-case scenarios, the elderly person can be inveigled or tricked into selling their family home, changing their will, or limiting their quality of life in ways that are unnecessary, given their resources. There is a profound psychological impact of this form of abuse. Understandably, the victims are likely to feel devastated when members of their family who they thought they could trust disappoint them. There is often a feeling of isolation because they can't rely on the people who surround them.

There are organisations, such as Seniors Right in Australia and Action on Elder Abuse in the UK, available to provide advice and support to victims of elder abuse. Discussing family finances with your adult children early in your retirement years, making a legal will, appointing a legal power of attorney (and choosing that person wisely), and acting early in cases where you (or other members of your family) suspect financial abuse are all strategies that may lessen the financial, emotional, and psychological impact of this traumatic experience.

FINANCIAL SECURITY OR FINANCIAL STRESS?

Not all retirees face financial stress after they retire. Some have accumulated sufficient savings in one form or another to last them what might be many years of retirement. But many others find themselves wondering how they will survive these years. Some may have a small nest egg to help; others may be wholly reliant on a (often inadequate) pension. We have seen that women, especially single women, are especially vulnerable, given their lower incomes over their working lives compared to men and their unstable careers due to factors like childrearing or caring for family members.

Clearly, we need to create policies that will change the gender pay gap and ensure retirement is not a stage of life during which financial stress governs the lives of many retirees. Looking at OECD data for pension policies across many countries, it's evident that one size does not fit all and that policies must be framed around each country's demographics and financial resources. Key concerns identified include increasing the retirement age, ensuring financial sustainability of pension systems, and providing a safety net for low-income earners. As OECD Director General Angel Gurría concludes about pension policy:

> Further reforms are needed that are both fiscally and socially responsible. We cannot risk a resurgence of old age poverty in the future. This risk is heightened by growing earnings inequality in many countries, which will feed through into greater inequality in retirement.[20]

A FEW TIPS ON MANAGING YOUR FINANCES

1. What will be your expenses post-retirement? Planning a budget for your retirement is not easy, but worth the effort. You may not need (or be able to) to spend as much on clothing, entertainment, or travel, but be prepared to budget for the possibility of increased health care costs and, as you age, the costs of services such as house cleaning and gardening. Power and communication bills are likely to increase, and of course inflation will always be a factor. Thinking about a budget will help you make decisions such as whether you would be best to work for a few more years or take up part-time work, pay for house repairs while you are still working, or consider downsizing your home.

2. What are your assets? Work out how much you have in savings, superannuation, and pension entitlements before you retire. Can you organise your post-retirement investments so that they are diversified, productive, relatively safe, and tax effective?

3. When you retire, don't spend too much too soon. It's tempting to take superannuation lump sums, but remember these funds may need to stretch out for many years. On the other hand, it can be a good idea to pay off your house mortgage as soon as possible if you haven't already done so. And if it's your dream to travel the world when you retire, better to do so while you're younger and healthier. If these issues are taxing you, one investment worth making is to consult an accredited financial advisor.

4. Stay alert to scams and frauds. Educate yourself about security procedures when you're banking, investing, making online purchases, or interacting with others online. Be sceptical of amazing bargains and offers, or emails/phone messages that are expressed as urgent. Change your passwords often. Have a trusted group you can ask if you're unsure – for example family members, your bank manager, or accountant.

5. Avoid STDs (sexually transmitted debts)! These can occur when an individual becomes responsible for all or part of their partner's financial debt, for example, if money is spent on a joint credit card without your agreement, or if you sign as guarantor for a loan your partner has organised and your partner defaults on payment. These situations can occur when a relationship ends, through partner coercion (or theft), or simply through miscommunication. In financial matters, make sure you understand what you are signing!

6. Stay engaged with your world. Keep alert, educate yourself about investments, and get advice about changes in government policies concerning retirees and the advantages and pitfalls of different investment schemes.

4

RETIREMENT, HEALTH, AND WELLBEING

You've worked hard for many years and now you are retired. All those stressors – gone! All that structure to your day – gone! All the effort of trying to fit too many tasks into one day – gone! How will this change affect your health and life expectancy?

It's complicated. When moving from work to non-work, everything about your daily schedule changes. You may be more relaxed, and your life may slow down. Loss of work-related stress may be a great relief and good for your health, but losing the daily structure and your work relationships can also be stressful and harmful to your health. In fact, retirement is ranked 10th on the list of life's most stressful events. Predicting how retirement affects health is extremely difficult because retirement goes hand in hand with ageing, and retirees are, for the most part, older than those still working. Thus, what might seem to be a consequence of retirement can be simply part of the ageing process. The relationship between retirement and health is an important one to consider given the shifting trends in labour force attachment, ageing of the population, and growth in the cost of health care.

As we mentioned earlier, there has been dramatic increase in life expectancy through the 20th century and, correspondingly, longer periods spent in retirement. The remarkable improvements in life

DOI: 10.4324/9781003611783-4

expectancy over the past century were part of a shift in the leading causes of disease and death. There is now considerable literature naming advances in medicine as one factor responsible for increased life expectancy, including the change in types of illness or disease from communicable diseases to – mostly – chronic, non-communicable diseases and disability. It is true that this trend was disrupted by the COVID epidemic in 2020/21 following which COVID became the second leading cause of death worldwide, after ischaemic heart disease. Nevertheless, even in low-income countries, heart disease and stroke still rank in the top ten causes of disease for older people.[1]

One major health consequence of a longer lifespan is the increase in prevalence of dementia. This places considerable demands on the health care system, on long-term care, and on wellbeing of family members, especially the primary carer. The World Health Organisation notes that the risk of dementia rises sharply with age with an estimated 25 to 30 per cent of people ages 85 years or older showing some evidence of this condition.

What do we know about health and retirement? Is finally quitting the workplace good for you or not?

RETIREMENT AND PHYSICAL HEALTH

Longitudinal studies are important to answer this question because they show changes over time rather than simply compare groups of retired and non-retired people who may well differ on other key variables such as age, type of occupation, lifestyle variables, and pre-existing conditions.

One large longitudinal study, across 12 Western European countries, using rigorous methods, showed that although health gradually declines in the retirement years due to ageing, in the short term, retirement can lead to improvements in self-reported health, across educational levels, and for men and women alike.[2] Giving up work is often accompanied by a decrease in stress, better sleep quality, and more time to exercise and maintain a healthy diet, all factors potentially associated with health improvements.

But it's a complex issue. A systematic review of 82 longitudinal studies examining the effects of retirement on cardiovascular disease (CVD) and its risk factors showed different results in different countries.[3] In the US there were no significant effects of retirement on CVD, while in European countries (except France), effects were detrimental to heart health. In relation to risk factors, those retiring from physically demanding jobs in the US and several European countries showed a significant tendency to put on weight post-retirement. Studies of other CVD risk factors for which adequate data was available (for example smoking and drinking alcohol) were inconsistent, many showing little or no change. A conclusion from this analysis is that the effect of retirement on CVD varies according to the health variables studied and the specific research population, a conclusion that underscores the complexity of the question.

A longitudinal study by Szabo and colleagues drilled down on some of these complexities through a sophisticated statistical analysis of three or more tranches of longitudinal data assessing the physical health of New Zealanders pre- and post-retirement.[4] Three different pathways of influence were delineated – those who showed slowly declining physical health post-retirement (slow decliners), those who generally maintained their pre-retirement health post-retirement (maintainers), and those whose health actually improved (improvers). Slow decliners were more likely than maintainers to have worked in a non-professional capacity, less likely to be partnered, more likely to smoke and to have multiple chronic conditions. Improvers were also more likely than maintainers to have multiple chronic conditions, and less likely to take on paid work post-retirement. The study authors concluded that retirement has physical health benefits for those whose working conditions are poor or who have pre-existing chronic conditions. For those who already rate themselves as healthy, extra physical health benefits are less likely.

One's financial, personal, and social resources are implicated in how retirement affects health and wellbeing. A longitudinal study of 118 Hong Kong Chinese pre- and post-retirement showed positive changes in wellbeing in those retirees whose resources increased after they had ceased working. Those who had favourably organised their retirement savings and investments, sought social support for this life phase, and engaged in regular exercise – that is, had made and implemented retirement plans – also self-reported increased wellbeing.[5]

WHAT INFLUENCES RETIREMENT HEALTH?

I did not expect retirement to be this good. I feel that I am fortunate to be in good health, and able to enjoy life as it is.

I expected my health to be better, and to be more mobile than I am. This is restricting me in many ways . . . I can no longer join friends for brisk walks, hikes with backpacks etc.

What is behind these two contrasting experiences of health in retirement? As shown in the research described previously, sometimes retirement leads to health improvements and sometimes it does not. Issues which may affect health outcomes include pre-existing conditions, social connectedness and support, participation in physical exercise, post-retirement lifestyle (e.g., changes in smoking or alcohol use), being partnered, finances, and the reason for retirement, for example, voluntary, due to illness, or due to dismissal/redundancy.

One thought-provoking link with poor health is the experience of loneliness and social isolation. While not specifically a problem of retirees, retirement may trigger increased loneliness through decreased social connections. There is strong evidence that social isolation and loneliness heighten the risk for premature mortality and that this risk exceeds that of many key ill-health indicators.[6] Researchers have shown that loneliness can be a bigger killer than obesity and should be considered a major public health issue. A review of 218 studies into the health effects of social isolation and loneliness[7] found that lonely people have a 50 per cent higher chance of premature death, while obesity increases the chance of early death by 30 per cent. The team found that the risk of early death associated with loneliness, social isolation, and living alone was equal to or greater than the premature death risk associated not only with obesity but with other major health conditions.

Another factor relates to lifestyle changes post-retirement. Some people improve their nutrition and exercise regimes; others do not. For example, in a large study of Australian women in 2016,[8] retirement status had positive effects on women's self-reported physical and mental health outcomes. These positive effects were linked to increased physical activity post-retirement and reduced smoking. Interestingly, a Finnish study demonstrated that while women tended to improve their dietary habits when they retired, this was not the case for retired men.[9]

A long-term study of British civil servants reinforces the need for caution in concluding that retirement affects health, either positively or negatively. On-time retirement and voluntary early retirement were both related to better physical functioning and mental health when retirees were compared to those who remained in the workforce. The authors suggested that there might be a causal relationship between voluntary retirement and positive health outcomes. However, we need here to consider the possibility of including selection bias. For example, those who choose earlier retirement may do so either because their health is compromised or because they are healthy and want to enjoy retirement activities while still fit enough to do so. Certainly, there is evidence from our study of Australian women that a significant minority retire voluntarily, but many do so for health reasons (15 per cent), because of work stress (19 per cent), or the ill health of family members (11 per cent). We need to tease out what is meant by 'voluntary' retirement.

Is early retirement a healthy idea? Some studies have shown that early retirement has negative consequences for post-retirement physical and emotional health and cognitive functioning, although, in respect of the last, there is recent evidence that work requiring higher mental demands is protective against cognitive decline, independent of education level and socio-economic status. At least one study has shown that people who retired at age 55 had almost twice the risk of earlier death compared to people who retired at age 60. The link between early retirement and early death was greater for men than women; men who retired at 55 had an 80 per cent greater increased risk than women who retired at 55.

There are many challenges with estimating the impact of retirement on health apart from the confounding of retirement with ageing as we have seen. The difficulty in establishing clear links between physical health and retirement suggests it may prove more productive to examine psychological health. The most commonly researched marker of mental health in retirement is depression, while another approach is to assess perceived wellbeing and life satisfaction post-retirement.

RETIREMENT AND PSYCHOLOGICAL WELLBEING

> I thought that I was ready to retire mentally – but found that it actually took me three years to adjust – I grieved for my job and that process took that long. There was no help or recognition about the grieving process. I had to work through that myself, and it was only after I came out the other end that I realized what had happened to me.

Psychological wellbeing refers to the extent to which an individual experiences life in a positive way and functions well psychologically. Our study of retired women measured two wellbeing measures – self-esteem and stress levels. When asked if their self-esteem was better, the same, or worse than before they retired, most reported 'same', while one quarter reported higher self-esteem post-retirement. In turn, higher levels of self-esteem were associated with significantly better health post-retirement, as well as greater satisfaction with their health. Three quarters of the study participants reported being less stressed, and only 7 per cent were more stressed after they retired.

Another measure of wellbeing is life satisfaction. A longitudinal study in Finland examined changes in life satisfaction during the retirement transition among over 3,000 aging public sector employees, who were followed up annually before and after retirement.

Life satisfaction improved among the entire study population during the retirement transition and remained stable thereafter. The improvement was greater for women than men, and for those with suboptimal health before retirement compared with those who had good health.[10]

What of depression in retirement? Depression is an important health problem in many countries. It reduces productivity at work and is the fastest increasing reason for early retirement. There is convincing evidence that depression is associated with increased likelihood of early retirement, and depressed individuals retire at a significantly younger age than those without depression. However, retirement can help to ameliorate depressive symptoms. A systematic review and meta-analysis encompassing over half a million research participants showed that retirement generally had a protective effect on mental health, reducing the risk of depression by nearly 20 per cent.[11] On the other hand, a different, but similarly large, meta-analysis of longitudinal studies of retirement drew contrasting conclusions. These researchers found that the transition to retirement was associated with a *higher* risk of depression. However, this trend was more pronounced among those whose retirement was involuntary, and among those retirees in Asian countries.[12] National differences may relate to factors such as differences in attitudes to work and ageing, as well as different economic and social circumstances experienced by retirees. There is no simple answer to the question as to how retirement affects mental or physical health, as so many factors are involved. What is perhaps a more fruitful exercise is to consider the circumstances that are most associated with post-retirement adjustment/wellbeing, and which factors are potential risks to good health.

PREDICTORS OF POST-RETIREMENT PSYCHOLOGICAL ADJUSTMENT

Psychological wellbeing and adjustment are greatly dependent on all the resources that individuals bring to the retirement transition. These resources can be personal, material, or social and are drawn on to help individuals manage stressful or difficult situations. While many (most?) retirees have little or no difficulty in negotiating retirement, some appear not to have the resources to refashion their lives. For example, in our study, the word 'boring' recurred frequently as women complained about the 'emptiness' of their retirement lives.

> It can be tedious, boring and even though I am a loner, more solitary than I would sometimes like. I don't fit much of the community programs and even some of the other activities that are around.

Lower levels of wellbeing are likely to result from external factors such as a partner's poor health or because of demanding family caring responsibilities, as these restrict opportunities to take up new roles in retirement. The gendered expectations of caring mean that women are more likely to regard caring for a partner as an obligation and spend more time doing so than men, a state of affairs that has been linked to increased stress.

Another concern for retirees who have spent many years in the workforce, with tasks clearly prescribed, is the lack of structure to their day.

> It's hard to build structure into a life that suddenly becomes freefalling.

Additionally, for those whose sense of self is tied to their work identity, retirement can be a daunting prospect. The lack of challenges and excitement that daily work brought to their lives is reflected in loss of self-esteem and sense of contributing to society.

> I absolutely hate it. I find it financially challenging, lonely and boring. I feel as though I am brain dead, and I am being left further and further behind in learning new technologies and discovering new interests. I find I am sinking into apathy and the less I do the less I want to do.

Recently, a number of studies addressing the determinants of adjustment to life during retirement have been published, reflecting the growing interest in this field. One thorough review[13] found physical health, adequate finances, psychological health, personality factors, engaging in leisure activities, retiring voluntarily, and social integration were key predictors. Factors not predicting adjustment in any consistent manner included age, sex, household composition, timing of retirement, and ethnicity. Specific personality factors associated with positive adjustment to retirement (and indeed to life in general) include agreeableness and conscientiousness, along with lower levels of neuroticism (as reflected, for example, in low self-esteem and high anxiety).[14]

The consequences of poor psychological wellbeing can be associated with retirees engaging in maladaptive behaviours. These behaviours can further compromise physical as well psychological wellbeing with implications for retirees' ability to plan and manage their retirement. As we have seen, some retirees miss the structure, the challenges, and the companionship of their working lives, and some find replacement activities that are problematic for their physical and mental health. Two of the most common behaviours are substance abuse (both alcohol and drugs) and problem gambling.

SUBSTANCE ABUSE AND GAMBLING

Even moderate alcohol consumption can have negative effects on health as one ages. In a recent large study of UK drinkers aged 60 and over, high risk drinking was associated with increased mortality through heart disease or cancer. Even among moderate or low risk drinkers, higher mortality rates were evident particularly for those who had other health-related risk factors or experienced socio-economic disadvantage.[15]

Despite this, in Australia in 2022–2023, one in three (33%) people aged 60 to 69 consumed alcohol at risky levels, similar to the alcohol consumption of people in their late 20s. Even among those aged 70 and over, 25 per cent were defined as risky drinkers (consumers of more than ten standard drinks per week on average, or more than four in a single day at least once a month).[16] US data show rates of alcohol abuse and dependence have increased with age, almost tenfold for women aged 65 and older, and fourfold for similarly aged men, over the last decade.[17] Why is this the case? Older individuals may be more susceptible to alcohol, tobacco, and other drug problems because of issues with pain management, boredom, loneliness/isolation, poor health, and difficulties coping with significant life events such as retirement.

Drug abuse among retirees and older people has focused largely on prescription drugs, by far the most common category of drug abuse among this group. Abuse of prescription drugs among older adults does not typically involve the use of these substances to 'get high', and the users do not usually obtain them illegally. Instead, unsafe combinations or amounts of medications may be obtained by seeking prescriptions from multiple doctors, by obtaining medications from family members or peers, or by stockpiling medications over time.

It is important to note, however, that substance abuse issues among the elderly represent a growing public health concern. According to 2017 data from the US Office of Alcoholism and Substance Use Services, 17 per cent of people over 65 in the US have abused prescription drugs. Clearly the link between retirement and abuse/overuse of alcohol and drugs, and the reasons for this, need to be a greater focus of attention by researchers.

In nations where there is ready access to gambling venues, excessive gambling can become a problem for retirees. An extensive review of the literature indicated that older adults are gambling more and more and that the proportion of pathological gamblers is increasing in this age group. Their motivations for gambling include entertainment, boredom, and loneliness, and it is interesting to note that pathological gambling among older adults is associated with medical, psychiatric, and social comorbidities.[18] A vicious circle can be created in which already disadvantaged older individuals increase their disadvantage through gambling addiction.

Excessive gambling, alcohol and drug use are maladaptive ways to cope with stress as in the long term they lead to further stress. For retirees who are finding difficulties making the transition from work to a non-working lifestyle, there are many healthy, adaptive options available, some of which we will discuss in this and subsequent chapters.

HOW TO MAINTAIN GOOD HEALTH IN RETIREMENT

How do we ensure good health in retirement? Sometimes retirement is a necessary outcome of poor health. Or the unexpected happens after we retire and we become ill in spite of all our efforts to remain healthy. Ageing itself is undeniably a health hazard. But there are some fundamental lifestyle choices that boost chances of a healthy retirement, both physically and mentally. It is important that pre- and post-retirement plans include taking care of yourself through healthy living. Here are some tips:

1. Maintain a healthy diet. Proper nutrition improves your energy levels, your resistance to illness and disease, and increases mental sharpness. Try to limit your intake of salt, unhealthy fats, and food with lots of additives. Eat plenty of fresh fruit and vegetables, reduce your alcohol intake as you age, and give up smoking. Find other ways to reward yourself if you are a 'comfort food' eater.
2. Get off the couch and get moving! Retirement provides the opportunity to engage in physical activity that may have been limited by the demands of full-time work. The positive link between retirement health and physical activity has been well documented. There are many ways to exercise without necessarily spending money on golf club or gym membership – find a community walking club or a neighbourhood Tai Chi group, leave the car in the garage and walk when you can, try chair yoga. You'll feel better and your mood will improve.
3. Get a good night's sleep. Some tips: limit daytime naps, avoid caffeine, alcohol, heavy meals, and computer screens before

bedtime; create a relaxing bedtime routine, arrange your bedroom environment to be comfortable, quiet, dark, and calm.

4. Have regular medical checks, especially for age-related diseases, as well as dental, optical, and especially hearing checks. It's difficult to maintain connection with others when your hearing is poor.

5. Exercise your brain; crosswords, puzzles, reading and learning new things are some of the activities that help you to maintain your level of cognitive functioning.

6. Stay connected. Your relationships with people can help you live longer. Nurture your friendships and family ties. If you are away from friends and family, think about making social connections in other ways such as through volunteering – it's a great way to meet people and get the health benefits of relationships too.

7. Look for a new sense of purpose. You might find this through volunteer work, grandparenting activities, an engaging hobby, or a new venture that you've always dreamt of doing.

5

RENEGOTIATING SOCIAL RELATIONSHIPS

Social relationships are bound to undergo significant changes when you retire. There are new friends to be made, old friendship to be resumed, workplace collegiality to be maintained and family relationships to be renegotiated. Both opportunities and potential pitfalls accompany the different social spaces that retirees occupy, and there may be need for adjustment of expectations and proactivity in developing new friendships. In this chapter, we discuss these relationship patterns and how they change during retirement.

INTIMATE PARTNER RELATIONSHIPS

Many surveys and studies have indicated that marital relationships either improve or stay the same when couples retire. There is more time for partners to do things together, carry out long-held plans and dreams, perhaps make a sea change or tree change, travel, or just relax. Intimacy can be enhanced, and couples may report that the depth of feeling for each other becomes even stronger as they share joys and sorrows of growing old together and watching their children and grandchildren mature. What about sex? Most people experience changes in their libido throughout life, but for many, a healthy sex drive will continue possibly for years post-retirement. The comforts

DOI: 10.4324/9781003611783-5

of touch and tenderness have no age limits. Research is clear that married/partnered retirees usually enjoy better psychological wellbeing than single or widowed retirees.[1]

It doesn't always work out this way. Partners spending so much more time together can discover they have far less in common than they realised when both were constantly busy with work and family. Expectations about activities in retirement, domestic responsibilities, and extent of 'togetherness' can turn out to be very different, with compromises difficult to achieve.

> I wish I had spent more time exploring my husband's vision of us in retirement. He saw it as us keeping each other company . . . and my being able to take back all the domestic chores. He doesn't like 'going out' and he doesn't like being left home alone . . . he sulks!

As well, in our studies, a number of women commented on the level of dependency shown by their spouse post-retirement.

> I find my husband needs me more than I need him. I can't go shopping without him coming or ringing to find out where I am and when I'll be home. This is hard to deal with as we were once both senior public servants and independent of each other.

Retired men can find developing new social networks more difficult than do women, who tend to be more socially integrated, possibly because many have spent significant periods of their adult life outside of the paid workforce and so are more likely to have developed non-work friendship groups. Although there are many individual differences in sociability, it seems that retired men too often isolate themselves. For example, a large-scale time-use survey in Australia found that paradoxically, retired men spent less time with family and friends outside of the household than men still in the workforce. Retired women were the opposite, making use of their time in retirement to socialise with family and friends from outside their immediate household.[2]

Unfortunately, the intimate bond between some couples does not survive retirement, leading to late life divorce or separation, a phenomenon increasing along with our lifespans (and the expectation of many healthy years post-retirement). Divorce among the over 50s is becoming more common. Unsatisfied spouses may choose to end their marriage when their adult children leave home, deciding it is now or never to fulfil their dreams. Coping with partnership breakdown and the change of lifestyle accompanying retirement can put a major strain on personal resources, financially and emotionally.

> My wife and I were together for 35 years, and our financial affairs were so intertwined that it took a full year to disentangle them and sort out who got what. That was the easy part. It's the loneliness and heartbreak that is hard to bear.

A different family issue but one that is not uncommon during retirement is the death of a partner. As well as the sadness of bereavement, the death of a spouse means the loss of so many day-to-day interactions and shared activities, increasing the risk of loneliness and depression. Retirees can struggle to cope, especially in the early years of grieving. Plans need to be re-evaluated during this vulnerable time.

> I expected to be sharing retirement with my husband of 40 years. However, he was diagnosed with Stage 4 cancer in 2014 and died 25 months later.

A partner's poor health and need for care also restricts opportunities to take up new roles in retirement. These situations are likely to be associated with changes to the nature of the relationship between the ill person and their carer, as well as the possibility of compromised wellbeing for the carer. Gendered expectations surrounding nurturance mean that women are more likely to regard caring for a partner as an obligation, and spend more time doing so than men, a state of affairs that has been linked to increased stress. We discuss further aspects of the carer role in the next section.

FAMILY RELATIONSHIPS

Expectations that retirement will allow for more and enriched family time are not always realised. The busy lives of your adult children are unlikely to have altered just because you have retired. Your son or daughter may not choose to spend their day off work with you; they have their own lives to lead. Your retirement and the ageing process that accompanies it can also lead to family conflicts about where you live and how you choose to spend your money.

Nevertheless, retirement does provide the opportunity to strengthen family relationships. Retirees, if they are able, can offer various forms of assistance to other family members, such as financial assistance, mentoring, help with chores and grandparenting duties. Research suggests this has reciprocal benefits. Retirees who regularly look after their grandchildren, or often help their children with practical tasks, experience more intergenerational support through their retirement transition compared with retirees who never provide these types of help.[3]

CARING FOR GRANDCHILDREN

For those who are lucky enough to have young grandchildren, assisting with babysitting and childcare can be a wonderful opportunity to create powerful bonds with the grandchildren as well as strengthen family relationships in general. In studies we have conducted, grandparents described many significant and life-enhancing benefits arising from their role, including a new focus for their love and a source of joy and pleasure.[4] Some retired specifically to spend more time with their grandchildren.

> Well, I was working full-time when Lily was born and I worked a nine-day fortnight so I could have a day with her. And then I took retirement early, so the kids had a big influence on that I think. They sort of showed me there was more to life than working. Now if I have the kids I can devote myself to them, I don't have to do a hundred other things at the same time.

In Chapter 2 we discussed the concept of 'generativity', the idea that a mature and healthy psychosocial development for one's middle and senior years involves contributing to the welfare of the next generation. Overall, the grandparents in our studies developed a stronger sense of generativity through their concern for, nurture, and guidance of their children and grandchildren. Other researchers have also noted the relationships between time spent looking after grandchildren, sense of generativity, overall satisfaction with life, and even extended lifespan.

Problems can occur when the expectations of retiree grandparents do not meet the expectations of parents. Sometimes the amount of childcare expected can be a cause for stress or conflict. One woman put it this way.

> One daughter expects me to come whenever she calls for babysitting even though it disrupts my own plans. It is expected of me as I am the non-working grandmother.

Particularly stressful can be the situation in which grandparents must assume the full-time carer role for their grandchildren, usually because of some difficult or tragic family situation such as parental death, illness, drug addiction, or criminality. In these cases, retirees can find themselves emotionally, physically, and financially challenged. Many – perhaps most – make the best of it for the sake of their grandchildren, and still find love and joy in the strength of their relationships. Nevertheless, such situations are certainly a challenge to retirement plans for 'me time'!

CARING FOR ELDERLY RELATIVES

Elderly relatives or one's partner may also need care. Because we are living longer, many retirees are likely to have frail or ill parents. Women typically spend more than twice the amount in caring duties than men (and, perhaps unsurprisingly, brothers defer to their sisters when parental care is needed). Studies show men and women who provide care for elderly family members report negative mental and physical health consequences, including a higher mortality rate. Indeed, the need to care for a partner or older relative can be an unanticipated outcome or a precipitator of retirement with the possible financial consequences that can accompany early retirement. Caring for the elderly can be challenging as these quotes illustrate.

> I am trapped – caring for a demanding and often aggressive elderly mother. I see no end in sight.

> All the planning in the world goes out the window when 'life' happens. My mother is 97. While she lives in supported accommodation, as her only relative in our town, I am her primary carer. All my plans to do a lot of walking travelling overseas just can't happen. That's life!!!!

Retirees who are full-time or even occasional carers for those who are elderly or ill are a vulnerable population. Even when the cared-for person is greatly cherished and easy to get on with, there are stresses to manage. Not the least of these is the eventual death of a loved partner, parent, or relative, with the subsequent grief – and sometimes guilt – that this can bring. Depression, poor physical health, exhaustion, loneliness, and social isolation are further risks of being a principal carer. Self-care is vital. Finding out what community resources are available, marshalling family and local support, taking time off by accessing respite care, maintaining supportive friendships, and keeping healthy are important considerations for any carer, whether retired or not.

THE SPECIAL CASE OF SINGLES

> Being alone and single [in retirement] is stressful, lonely and embarrassing and socially limiting.

> Retirement brings with it (for me anyway) loneliness, poverty, social isolation that I do not relish. A 'single' status where everything is twice the cost. No other income to rely on other than

what you generate yourself. No partner to share life's problems with or do anything for you. Single limited income to pay for maintenance and repairs.

Demographic trends in Western nations suggest that a rising share of unpartnered people will be entering retirement age in the near future. These may be the never married, widows and widowers, or divorced people who have not re-partnered. There is clear evidence that singles living alone, particularly the never married, experience economic and health disadvantages in retirement. This is the case for both men and women. A major US review presents data to indicate that the never married have the largest share of persons aged 65 or over living in poverty (nearly 22 per cent), compared to 4.5 per cent of married persons, 17 per cent of the divorced, and 14.5 per cent of widows/widowers. Singles living alone must rely on one income and do not have the benefits of pooling resources or economies of scale available to those sharing a household; for example, it costs the same to heat a house regardless of how many live there.[5]

An example of this level of disadvantage is shown in a longitudinal study in which 1,000 older citizens of Melbourne, Australia, were followed up for 16 years. At the beginning of the study, three quarters of the sample said they wanted to stay in their homes, with help, when they could no longer cope with independent living. Only 5 per cent said they preferred to move to an aged care facility. However, after 16 years, 17 per cent had moved into such a facility, despite their preferences. Being single was a risk factor for non-preferential moving to an age care residence, as were being a woman, renting (that is, not owning your own home), and depression.[6]

Marriage and cohabitation proffer health advantages as well as financial benefits. Married people live longer on average than the unmarried, and never married men have particularly high mortality rates. For the over 65s, health-related restrictions on daily activities and physical inactivity rates are higher in the never married than the married, with rates for divorced and widowed people falling in between. Why is this so? Speculations include the idea of 'marriage protection' (marriage is associated with social approval and promotes healthier habits) and the 'marriage selection bias' (healthier people with more adaptive lifestyle habits are more likely to get married in the first place).

As is illustrated by the quotes at the beginning of this section, singles are also more likely to become socially isolated once they leave the workforce. Living alone is a risk factor, one that is exacerbated by health and financial limitations on activities. Of course, not all unmarried or never married people live alone, and not all those who live alone are lonely. Differences in temperament, family and friendship networks, and social opportunities all mitigate the risk of loneliness and isolation. For example, a group of single women retirees we are aware of have moved to apartments in the same building so they can assist each other as they age. They arrange regular outings and meals together but retain the privacy of their own living spaces. Others talk about the active efforts they have made to manage a satisfying retirement lifestyle as a single, as in the following example.

> I have several close friends who are also single and who retired around the same time as me, and therefore we have been a support for each other in some ways. I have always been very busy both in work and with life in general, I have always had a positive outlook on life, and I believe retirement is enabling me to focus more on my personal desires rather than workplace issues.

NEW INTIMACIES

As we have noted, singles, divorcees, and widows/widowers may be particularly vulnerable to loneliness and social isolation when they retire. It is not surprising that new partnerships are sought or formed in these retirement years. An issue for retirees seeking intimate partners is that they are no longer as well connected to workplace networks, which usually provide opportunities to meet people. One solution is to go online.

Dating websites, apps, or social media have proliferated in recent years, and older people, no less than young, see these as a means of finding companionship and romance. While some potential partners are genuine, there are those whose pretence of being a prospective companion is a ploy. Newspapers and other media abound with stories of retirees using these services who have been victims of fraud or scammed in some way. Victims report financial exploitation, pervasive lying, and unwanted sexual aggression, among other negative experiences. So why do older women and men use these sites? Expanding their social networks, for friendship and romance, and knowing more about one's partner are benefits of online dating reported by older dating site users. Scammers can play on triggers such as these to entice people to provide money, gifts, or personal details. But sadly, as well as the financial price there is also an emotional cost for those looking for love online when the scam becomes evident. With appropriate care and safeguards, online dating and friendship sites may lead to the formation of successful and long-lasting relationships. Even if they do not fulfil this purpose, such sites offer the opportunity to meet interesting people and remain socially engaged, as long as they are approached with due caution. Not everyone met online is a scammer!

WORKPLACE SOCIALISING

Peer group socialising and friendships also undergo change when we retire. One of the functions of many workplaces is that they provide social connections. These can be quite extensive, including not just day-to-day interactions but a range of after-work social opportunities and events. In some cases, close friendships are formed, but even when this does not occur, there are usually people around in most workplaces to have a cup of coffee or a chat with. As well as colleagues, customers come and go during the day, providing interest and social interaction – someone to talk to and perhaps something to talk about. When we asked retirees what they missed most about work, many mentioned friends and colleagues.

> [I missed] being with work colleagues who are friends willing to listen and also to be listened to in supportive ways.

> I miss the camaraderie of my workmates.

Once you have retired, it is more difficult to maintain relationships with workplace colleagues, who will still be busy during the working day. Close workplace friendships may suffer when there is not the opportunity to catch up on a daily basis, and special 'dates' or telephone calls cut into the family time of those still working. Many acquaintances and casual friendships will not be renewed. Of course, many retirees do maintain active friendships with former colleagues who become a strong part of their post-retirement social group. For most though, already existing non-work friendship circles will become more salient, and there will be a challenge to join new groups and make new friendships of fellow retirees. Nevertheless, the risk of loneliness and social isolation, discussed next, is real.

SOCIAL CONNECTEDNESS AND LONELINESS

Loneliness has been described as an epidemic, particularly among the elderly. Recent research indicates that nearly 30 per cent of those aged 60 and above experience some degree of loneliness, with rates even higher among the over 75s and those living in care homes. What's more, loneliness and social isolation are linked to higher rates of heart disease, stroke, diabetes, dementia, and depression, as well as an increased risk of premature death of about 26 to 29 per cent. How does this happen? One explanation is that loneliness and social isolation lead to the neglect of self-care (through, for example, poor diet, substance misuse, and low utilisation of health services) plus heightened stress levels associated with poorer mental health.[7]

A headline from an article in the UK-based *Telegraph* newspaper, 'Wanted: Job for lonely widower (89) bored of retired life', is a poignant reminder of the extent to which loneliness can be a risk factor for the retired and elderly. With positive marital relationships one of the strongest protective factors against loneliness, the newly widowed are particularly vulnerable. What is missing from the lives of lonely people? A survey of over 65s by the UK's Campaign to End Loneliness found it was often those simple and ordinary interactions we too readily take for granted – like sitting with someone, laughing with someone, having a hug, or sharing a meal. One 87-year-old man described his loneliness as like a 'heavy cloud' hanging over him.[8]

A strong intimate partnership, higher education, and income are protective factors against loneliness, as is personal temperament. Although events like widowhood can increase feelings of aloneness, on the whole this feeling does not change much throughout life. People who have never felt particularly lonely are more likely to eventually bounce back from setbacks like widowhood (which is, of course, not to underestimate its impact). The lonely widower in the newspaper article had already used some positive coping strategies to improve his life. Most importantly, he has asked for help and support.

Independent risk factors for loneliness include being male, physical health symptoms, chronic work and/or social stress, small social network, lack of a spousal confidant and poor quality social relationships.[9] Those who are ill or stressed have fewer resources to develop or maintain friendships; for example, they may lack mobility to visit others or attend clubs and interest groups. Smaller social networks are susceptible to further reduction as friends move location, become less mobile themselves as they age, or eventually die. As we saw in a previous section, men's socialising is stereotypically more activity based and less intimate than women's, a style that means that men's friendship groups may be more susceptible to disbanding when life changes like retirement or the disabilities of ageing occur.

An important factor mitigating against loneliness is social connectedness. This has been described as having a sense of belongingness to a social group, a group in which there is trust, shared purpose, and mutual obligation. Lack of social connectedness differs from loneliness, as it is possible to be socially connected to others yet still feel lonely or to be socially isolated yet contented. Nevertheless, social isolation and loneliness are strongly related for most people. Many studies indicate the physical and psychological health benefits of social connectedness. It is a resilience factor that assists in coping with the ups and downs of day-to-day life, including the retirement transition and the changes of ageing. The socially connected experience more companionship, have more activity options to alleviate boredom, and have a larger circle to call on in times of stress or trouble. A review of nearly 150 studies found that those who reported lower levels of social connection had a greater risk of early death than those who smoked, drank, or were obese.[10] Although loneliness is a risk factor for poor health outcomes, there is debate about whether the lack of social connectedness is the more powerful factor, especially in relation to cognitive decline.[11]

In one interesting study, a group of UK seniors was followed across the first six years of retirement. A questionnaire measured their social group membership and quality of life at retirement and again six years later. Mortality over the period of the study was monitored. Social group memberships of the sample ranged widely, including, for example, book clubs, sporting teams, trade unions, and religious study groups. Retirees who were members of more social groups following their transition to retirement – and who retained these memberships post-retirement – had better quality of life and greater longevity than those with fewer or less long-lasting group memberships. These patterns were not evident among a matched group of seniors who did not retire during the time of the study, suggesting to the authors that group membership had 'a distinct role to play in the process of adapting to new circumstances following retirement' (p. 6). What's more, these effects on both quality of life and longevity were comparable in size to those of physical activity, a well-established factor in maintenance of health during the senior years.[12]

Retiring from the workplace can certainly heighten the risk of losing social connectedness. A significant number of those retirees we surveyed reported that loneliness or social isolation were the worst aspects of retirement for them. As one said, 'At first I felt very isolated and lonely and all I wanted to do was curl up in a ball and cry'. This woman set to work on her social connections, joined several clubs in her area and turned her situation around, finally being able to say, 'I now have a new group of friends and am enjoying a great number of activities'.

Social isolation among seniors can negatively affect physical and mental health, increase mortality risk, and contribute to cognitive decline. It can lead to retirees becoming more vulnerable to scams and other forms of elder abuse.[13] It is a clear health risk. What strategies can help to alleviate social isolation and its consequences?

OVERCOMING LONELINESS AND SOCIAL ISOLATION

1. Set up some new social arrangements. You might arrange regular get-togethers with other retirees or former colleagues, increase your commitment to already existing friendship groups, join a club, take up a hobby that involves interacting with others, or try one of the suggestions in the next section.
2. Volunteering is good for you and good for others. It gives you the chance to work toward a common and worthwhile goal, to make new friends and to increase social connections.
3. Join a service club – it's a way to combine volunteering with social, sporting, and educational activities. There is ample research showing that civic engagement can offset role losses consequent on retirement.[14] Examples are Probus, Rotary, and the Men's Shed movement.
4. Learn something new. Taking classes in something you have always wanted to do or further developing a skill or knowledge base you already have is a great way to meet like-minded people. And it's good for you![15]
5. Do an exercise class, or yoga, Pilates, or play a sport. Group exercise classes for seniors are particularly effective and have the added bonus of increasing fitness and flexibility.
6. Get a job. If you're fit and healthy enough, part-time or even full-time work, perhaps in a different area, might be right for you (and a way to meet new people).
7. See what your local council and library have to offer, such as book groups, walking groups, coffee clubs, or classes like technology updates or crafts.
8. Change your living arrangements. Not for everyone, but group-based living is another possible way to overcome social isolation. Some retirees move in with their children or other relatives to

form multi-generational households. These offer many social and financial benefits but can strain family relationships if expectations are not mutual and boundaries not respected. Retirees who are single, widowed, or divorced sometimes group together with like-minded friends to share housing or live in neighbouring apartments. Leisure activities, daily chores, and expenses may be shared. When these situations work well, group members assist and support each other in difficult times, but again, it is important that all group members have clear expectations and contingencies, such as serious illness, have been thought through. Retirement villages are yet another form of group living that can provide social activities, connections, and support for retirees. While many articles have been written about potential pitfalls of retirement villages (particularly financial issues), they clearly work well for some. Suggestion: try before you buy!

9. Get a pet. A dog or other pet can provide company, exercise, and the chance to meet and chat to other humans through joining a club or just going for a walk. There is ample research that pet ownership is associated with greater wellbeing in older adults and that one of its effects is to mitigate loneliness.[16]

The key message here is that maintaining social contacts post-retirement is vital to health and wellbeing. For many, it will require purposive effort to guard against the unhealthy possibility of social isolation.

6

RESHAPING IDENTITY IN RETIREMENT

What do you do? It is a common conversation starter, signifying not only the social value of work, but the way in which one's job role is often viewed as a marker of social status and, quite possibly, attitudes to the world. Whether your response is doctor, teacher, clerk, mechanic, or any other job or profession, the expectation is that you identify with the norms of that work role. Your job title tells people something about *you*, not just the job you do. It is part of your identity. So what message does 'I'm retired' give? In this chapter, we discuss the psychological readjustment to our sense of self that occurs during the retirement journey.

RETIREMENT AS AN IDENTITY DISRUPTER

What do we mean by psychological identity? A sense of identity has been described as having an understanding of who you are and what matters to you, of having some clarity about your life goals and purposes. In the developmental psychology literature, adolescence is considered the key life stage at which we develop an adequate sense of identity. Failure to do so results in the uncommitted apathy of role confusion. Pathways that include choice of, and success in, roles that are socially valued and purposeful provide the most normative route

DOI: 10.4324/9781003611783-6

toward identity development. For adolescents, that typically means choosing a course of study, job, or career that has personal meaning and leads toward a functional adult life. Theorists have postulated that an 'identity crisis' is a defining feature of adolescence, as young people struggle to find this direction in life.[1]

By the time we get to our middle and senior years, identity is considered to be relatively stable and role confusion unlikely. We know who we are and where we are going, most of the time anyway. For many, if not most adults, a significant aspect of our identity relates to the work we do. Paid work is a key role in life, not only because of the time we spend in this role. Jobs provide status and social feedback. Work also makes an important contribution to our sense of self by enabling us to take on other adult roles, such as providing for a family or being perceived as a responsible community member (rather than a 'lay-about' or 'dole cheat').

For some, retirement creates a new identity crisis. While the core of a stable identity may well be an outcome of maturing from adolescent to adult, it is certainly true that any major life change can lead to questioning one's identity, with a consequent need to readjust and re-negotiate roles and life purposes. Marriage, parenthood, divorce, migration, and retirement are all examples of life-changing events that will lead to modifications in one's sense of self, a process that may trigger anxiety and stress in some, excitement in others, and a mix of emotions in most. As roles are added or lost, aspects of identity may be disrupted or strengthened to form a different and more complex whole. The extent to which there is psychosocial 'crisis' during this process is likely to depend on the size, nature, and speed of the life change, the extent of attachment to the work role, one's temperament, the availability of social support, and the extent to which other desirable roles are carried over or forthcoming. In previous chapters, we presented evidence to show that retirement satisfaction and adjustment are linked to many different variables, including the opportunity to plan and choose when to retire and the extent to which social support and connectedness is available to the retiree. Let us now consider the influence of worker identity on managing the retirement transition.

WORKER IDENTITY AND RETIREMENT ADJUSTMENT

We asked participants in our large sample study of retired women, 'What do you miss most about working?'[2] While many said 'nothing' or 'the money', a significant number of responses were couched in terms of the role of work in identity and meaning making.

> [I miss] feeling worthwhile. I think I'm of the generation who sees my value in terms of the job I do. I feel I have lost my identity.

> [I miss] the identity and recognition I received, and the sense of purpose/worth achieved by the challenges of work.

Others said 'I feel invisible', 'I've lost my sense of purpose', or 'I miss making a contribution'.

We also asked these women their reasons for working, giving them the opportunity to rate as 'very important', 'important', or 'not important' ten different work motives. Some reasons were considered stronger indicators of a tendency to shape personal identity around workplace activities and goals. These included acknowledging that work 'makes a contribution to my sense of who I am', 'contributes to my self-esteem', 'provides intellectual stimulation', and 'gives me a sense of making a contribution'. In our well-educated sample, a large percentage of respondents considered each of these reasons for working were very important (56, 52, 69, and 60 per cent respectively). We used these items to develop a measure of worker identity and found that those who had retired from occupations of professional and managerial status scored significantly higher on this aspect of identity than those who retired from occupations to which lower status was attached. Similarly, higher levels of education were associated with stronger worker identity. In these findings, we simply replicated a general consensus of organisational psychology research – those in socially valued occupations and/or occupations requiring longer and more committed training are more likely to view their work role as a significant aspect of their sense of self. This is true for both men and women.

Strength of worker identity was associated with adjustment to retirement. As might have been predicted, those with stronger ties to their work role expressed less satisfaction with their retirement than those with weaker ties. This was a statistically significant effect, albeit a quite small one. There were many individual differences, even among the strongly work attached, in the extent to which dissatisfaction with retirement was expressed. For example, it partly depended on how long the women had been retired. Dissatisfaction was more likely among those who had recently relinquished their paid work roles. Those retired for longer periods had more time to adjust and were consequently more comfortable with their role as retiree. Other factors which modified the effect of worker identity were number of activities participated in during retirement and satisfaction with social connectedness. Those who had taken on a larger variety of roles post-work, and those who perceived they were more socially connected, were more likely, in time, to overcome the negative feelings associated with the loss of their work role. Similar findings that have been replicated for both men and women in several recent studies.[3]

These are not surprising results. The 'workaholic', that is, those committed to their jobs who spend long hours at work or thinking about it, have less time to develop responsibilities in the community, get to know their neighbours, maintain and nurture their friendships, or enjoy hobbies and interests. They need time to process their change of status, experiment with new roles, and channel their passions in new directions. As we saw in Chapter 2, retirement is a psychosocial journey, not simply a change of state.

Findings from previous research about the association between worker identity and retirement adjustment are equivocal. Some show a positive relationship of worker identity with retirement adjustment, while others, like ours, show a negative relationship.[4,5] This variation in outcomes is likely to be for at least two reasons. First, different outcome measures have been employed across different studies, for example self-esteem, retirement adjustment, or life satisfaction. We found a negative effect of worker identity on retirement satisfaction, but no association with overall life satisfaction, indicating that worker identity does not necessarily have pervasive effects. A second issue is that there are so many factors influencing retirement adjustment and not all studies control for all of these. We found effects of worker identity diminished over time, and others have also shown that the longer you are retired, the less likely that influences from your working days will affect current adjustment.[5] Different factors take over, such as strength of friendships and enjoyment of new activities. Recent Australian and US research shows that post-retirement adjustment is convincingly related to the number and intensity of retirees' non-work identities, as reflected either in their self-described central life roles (e.g., grandparent, volunteer, committee member) or their group memberships.[6]

A concept called 'older worker identity' has been postulated as influential in the ease or difficulty of adjusting to retirement. Older worker identity describes a set of self-beliefs regarding one's diminishing capacity, because of age, to successfully manage occupational tasks. Examples of items in an Older Worker Identity Scale include 'I am less effective in accomplishing my work', 'I have become less creative in accomplishing my work', 'I am no longer motivated to accomplish my tasks', and 'I have become less adaptable and flexible'.[7] Interestingly, while older worker identity relates to intention to retire in several studies, it is not shown to improve retirement adjustment.[8] This may be because it comprises a rather negative set of beliefs about ageing and performance. Retiring because of feeling less able and competent imbues this stage of life with less positive overtones than retiring to achieve new goals.

GENDER DIFFERENCES

Early studies of retirement adjustment concluded that men had more difficulties in managing this transition than women, because their occupational attachments (or worker identities) were stronger and because they had weaker social networks and fewer 'non-work routines' (by which was meant domestic and community duties).[9] Such research does not take into account the strong growth in women's employment in the last 20 to 50 years or of women's improved representation in higher status jobs. More recently there have been some suggestions that it is women who will find the transition more difficult because they are likely to retire having achieved fewer work goals (including financial security) than men. This postulated state of affairs is said to be a result of women's typical work patterns, which involve breaks in employment and generally lower status jobs.

Although there is no shortage of commentary and opinion on possible gender differences in both worker identity and retirement adjustment, up-to-date evidence is sparse. One qualitative interview study of retirees (22 men and 26 women) aged 50 to 65 years found 'traditional gender roles predominated', with men more likely to experience negative emotions on retirement and more likely to have viewed their work role as central to their identity. For example, one man described how he felt identity loss, anger, and a diminution of his (and his family's) status in the community when he was made redundant, even though he was financially secure, able to find bridging employment, and had many interests outside work. While these reactions were more common among the men, some women experienced them as well, for example, one female teacher who was constrained to retire at 60 likened her feelings to a grief reaction, a kind of bereavement for a lost self. Nevertheless, the study authors concluded that because of the predominance of traditional gender roles among the sample, the men they interviewed found the transition to retirement more difficult, as it stripped away an important aspect of what they perceived to be their masculine identity. Home-based, domestic roles and leisure pursuits did not adequately compensate for this loss.[10]

In a qualitative study, 34 male professional engineers aged 55 to 77 years were interviewed to talk about their late-stage career development.[11] Although not specifically asked about retirement, many spoke of it, mostly using negative language, such as 'problem' or 'trouble'. They foresaw financial worries, social isolation (going from 'talking to 60 people a day to talking to the cat'), a lack of other interests to fill their time, fear of ageing ('closing the gate, being put out to pasture'), and significantly, loss of identity ('I will no longer have the voice my position gives me'; 'You still seem to need something that preserves your worth'). In the later stages of their careers, these engineers had shaped their identities around being wise elders and knowledge custodians, people of purpose and value. They struggled with a belief that ageing and retirement would negate their contributions and thus, their worth as a person. A sense of indignation, and to some extent fear of the future, was palpable ('They wash their hands of you').

A couple of studies have focused on retired professional women, possibly to ascertain whether they have similar difficulties to work-identified men through the retirement journey. In one such study, 14 retired professional women, aged 64 to 82 years and who had retired between 7 and 15 years ago, were each interviewed twice. The aim was to examine how these women managed their retirement transition, particularly their process of renegotiating identity and life roles.[12] Several reflected on how they had experienced 'rolelessness' when they first retired and had initially struggled to find new life purposes. However, the majority did not report continuing disruption to their sense of self or identity. One woman nicely encapsulated this general finding:

> I always thought of myself as a person, as not just an occupation. Some people, they are an occupation and that's it. But ah, I had enough things that I was interested in and wanted to do that it didn't change.[13]

The women adopted three strategies to maintain the integrity of their self-concepts. First, they expressed strong, often multifaceted, pre-retirement self-concepts. Several noted the importance of their non-work roles, such as family, community, and friendship roles.

Second, 13 of the 14 women continued to practise their professional skills in one way or another post-retirement. They stated or implied that this continuity helped maintain their sense of competence. Finally, many of the study participants emphasised the value of discovering new skills and interests once retirement allowed them the time to do so. In fact, all the women had practised 'role expansion', substituting the loss of their professional roles with alternative roles such as volunteer work, board membership, mentoring, or part-time/casual work in their previous field (for example as a substitute teacher).

While the women in this study were aware of identity disruption as a potential outcome of retirement from their professional occupations, they took active steps to maintain a robust sense of self through both holding on to aspects of their pre-retirement personas and embracing new opportunities to expand their roles and goals. Very similar findings emerged from another small, in-depth interview study of professional women, which found that when these women retired, they engaged in psychological 'work' to re-negotiate new identities as retirees. Strategies included the carry-over of key elements of worker identity into retirement (for example sense of competence), developing new roles through volunteering and helping others, continuing to learn new skills, and focusing on the nurture of social networks.[14]

It seems there is a need for further research on the role of gender in retirement adjustment. First, there is a research gap in examining the characteristics and identity-restructuring strategies used by men who are successful, satisfied retirees. Second, replication of some of the early large-scale gender difference studies is needed to reflect the modern-day working environment of (somewhat) greater equality between the sexes.

ONCE A WORKER, ALWAYS A WORKER?

In this chapter so far, we have discussed how one's sense of identity can be disrupted by leaving behind the worker role and how that disruption can have effects on retirement adjustment. We have described some of the strategies that retirees use to redefine themselves and modify their identities as retired persons. In this section, we step back a bit with the reminder that worker identity can, and often does, remain a significant and healthy part of retiree self-definition. For example, in answering the question we posed at the beginning of the chapter, 'What do you do?', many retirees will answer, 'I'm a retired teacher/doctor/manager/electrician'. This self-description often goes beyond simply naming a past role, it implies something about present retirement activities. The next part of such a self-description is likely to fall into one of two categories. The first is an explanation of how the old role has been incorporated into the new, for example, 'I'm a retired teacher still doing casual teaching/volunteering as an English language teacher for new migrants/setting up a tutoring business'. The second is an explanation of how the old role has been left behind and a new, different role has taken its place, for example, 'I'm a retired teacher who is now an art student/who's setting up a travel agency/who is writing a novel about space ships'.

As retirement researchers Reitzes and Mutran put it, 'Retirees still think of themselves in terms of their former careers. Even when they no longer occupy the role, their identity lingers'.[15] Sense of self in retirement is forged from a mix of new and old roles.

A Swiss study of 792 persons aged 58 to 70 years, 443 of whom had retired and 349 who had not done so, addresses this issue of lingering worker identity.[16] A major aim was to examine how retired people's self-image differs from that of workers. Participants were asked to rate the importance of different self-description domains such as professional and family roles. Results indicated that the professional domain remained just as important for self-description to retirees as it was for those still working. In general, retired respondents were more 'identity diverse', rating more domains of self-description as important than did the not-yet-retired respondents. No domain of self-description became less important after retirement. Additionally, high identity diversity correlated with high life satisfaction. The more roles seniors assessed as important to them, the happier they were, either as workers or retirees.

There are various strategies that retirees use to maintain the salience of their worker identity. Which ones are deemed most attractive by retirees will depend on the type of job and the type of workplace from which they retired. For example, home-based workers in retirement might still occasionally accept a paid or unpaid contract but may be less likely to attend social events associated with their former career. Those who found a high level of intellectual stimulation in their former occupation are more likely to keep reading about progress and process in that field than those who were less cognitively involved. In our own study, the most common strategies used were reading about developments and changes in one's former field or place of work (41 per cent did this often, 45 per cent sometimes) and maintaining friendships with former work colleagues (34 per cent often, 49 per cent sometimes). About one-quarter of participants maintained links through attending social events (such as Christmas parties) at their former workplace, approximately 20 per cent went to talks or meetings associated with the field in which they had worked, and a similar proportion continued active membership of their professional association or union. A greater number, about 36 per cent, sometimes or often continued to do unpaid work in their area of expertise, for example mentoring or giving talks, while 18 per cent were casually employed in paid work from time to time. In short, retirees maintained work identity through both informal social links and more formal structural links; they utilised skills and contacts gained over their working life in contributing to their new identities.[17]

We measured 'workplace attachment' by combining participant ratings on the items described previously to form a scale and examined the associations between scale scores and several other variables. We found that those with professional or managerial jobs, or stronger worker identities before they retired, not surprisingly, had higher workplace attachment scores post-retirement. Workplace attached retirees were more highly educated and more active, in the sense that they engaged in a greater range of social and leisure pursuits than those who were less inclined to keep alive the links with their former occupations. Finally, they were more generative, expressing a greater satisfaction with their lifetime social and community contributions. It seems that workplace attachment strategies provided a path toward negotiating the retirement transition.

Workplace attachment declined as length of retirement increased (and people aged). This tendency was reflected in the way workplace attachment related to overall satisfaction with life. Those who were more workplace attached were generally more satisfied, but this only applied to the first ten years of retirement. Retirees – even those who strongly maintain their worker identity through continuing links with their workplace and/or former career – tend to gradually replace these links or let them drop out over time, without diminution of general satisfaction. Presumably, other (or fewer) activities replace workplace contacts and interests.

MANY PATHWAYS

As we noted earlier in the chapter, worker identity is stronger among those in professional and higher status occupations. It is also likely to be stronger for those who have not, in their working life, maintained what is often termed a 'work/life balance'. However, those who 'work to live' rather than 'live to work' are also likely to structure their sense of self in part around the roles that paid work provides, for example a contributor to social order, a breadwinner, a friendly colleague, a union member. On retirement, adjustments to these roles, and therefore sense of self, will still be required. They will be different for the neurosurgeon and the council worker, the teacher and the prison guard, the home-based IT worker, and the manager of a large corporation, but they will be adjustments, nonetheless.

Post-retirement psychological readjustments can involve maintenance and adaptation of one's worker identity in ways that have been discussed already in this chapter. But reshaping worker identity is only one of the pathways to the re-establishment of identity in retirement. For some, it is not an option because retirement will mean severing of most or all ties with the workplace. For some it will not be desirable because they neither enjoyed their work nor found it fulfilling.

That being so, retirement still offers many satisfying opportunities for renewal, such as allowing the time to focus on new and already established interests and hobbies, give back to the community, strengthen family ties or work through a 'bucket list' of desired activities.

Pathways to reshaping identity can and do take many directions and are likely to include periods of experimentation with some successes and some failures. Not all new activities and roles tried out will be sustained, not all friendship overtures will be fulfilling. Nevertheless, research is strong on the importance of social connectedness and the maintenance of social roles for retirement wellbeing (see Chapter 5). Developmental psychologists theorise that generative roles will be the most rewarding in one's middle and senior years, and that these will contribute to a stronger and more contented sense of self. These are roles that involve giving back to the community (for example through volunteering), fostering personal creativity, or investing in future generations (for example through mentoring the young or caring for grandchildren). While worthy, these roles are not available to all. No doubt a significant proportion of retirees are satisfied to shape a new identity around relaxation, leisure and social contact, to 'be' rather than constantly need to 'do'.

QUICK TIPS

1. Give some pre-retirement thought to the different work and non-work roles that you hold. Which ones are central to your sense of who you are? Which of your non-work roles can you maintain or strengthen when you retire?
2. If your work role has been important to your identity, can you continue some aspects of that role in retirement? For example, might you consider part-time or casual work, joining a profession-based retiree group, mentoring young people, or even writing your memoirs?
3. Be prepared to experiment. Using your skills in new ventures and putting energy toward maintaining your work-based social groups is one pathway; another is learning new skills and joining

new social groups. Yet another is to extend your pre-retirement non-work roles once you retire, giving them more time and emphasis. Family roles and your hobbies and interests fit this category. Some of these strategies to identity adaptation will be sustainable and satisfying, others less so. Be flexible.

4. Ideally, retirement will give you time to try some of those things you always wanted to do. Start planning now!

7

THE NEXT STAGE

OLD AGE

In this chapter we consider 'the next stage', the one that follows your adjustment to retirement or your decision to keep working well past the average retirement age. For want of better words, we'll call this 'old age', starting at about 80 years – sooner for some, later for others. When you reach 80, some of you might be still working, but most will have already retired, had 5, 10, or even 20 years to adjust to a new identity as 'retiree' and, hopefully, enjoy the fruits of your labour. For many, these are the best years of their lives![1]

If you've reached these senior years and you're still reasonably content with life, interested in the world, and managing the tasks of everyday living, consider yourself blessed. But be aware, once you enter your late 70s or early 80s, there will be challenges. Whereas you may not have felt old up until now, the limitations of ageing eventually begin to assert themselves. Your psychosocial task becomes maintaining quality of life, and that means making adjustments, drawing on your strengths, and finding ways that work for the new 'old you' to retain a sense of purpose and fulfilment.

DOI: 10.4324/9781003611783-7

LOSSES AND GAINS OF OLD AGE

Sadly, ageing is a risk factor for disease and disability. Life span is not the same as good health span! As people live longer, their risk of heart disease, dementia, reduced mobility, sensory impairments, and falls increases.[2] Awareness of these risks changes our behaviours; for example, as one's sight deteriorates and reaction time slows, we might decide it is safer to give up driving. Indeed, often it is our children or medical practitioners who decide this for us. We lose a significant aspect of our independence and must either find new ways to manage day to day activities like shopping, appointments, and social visits, or rely on others to help us. The result can be a significant curtailment of some of these activities, especially those related to socialising. Similarly, communication with others can be limited by hearing losses, while reduced energy and mobility problems lead to abandonment of once favourite pastimes like playing golf, walking, social groups, or attending the theatre or concerts. Mild memory impairment and forgetfulness is considered a relatively normal aspect of ageing and does not necessarily indicate the development of dementia, but even these mild losses can lead to social withdrawal. Older people may experience embarrassment or discomfort at not feeling on top of things in social situations. It is uncomfortable having your sentences finished for you because you hesitate over a word that has not quite come to the surface! A negative cycle can eventuate in which we find ourselves withdrawing from the world, a situation that can contribute to depression and loneliness.

Social withdrawal in turn becomes a risk factor for further impairments, for example, social isolation is one of the well-established modifiable risk factors for dementia.[3] The Alzheimer's Society estimates that about 11 per cent of UK citizens in the 80–85 age group and 33 percent aged 90 or older are diagnosed with this condition, and as the 'cure' is still elusive, it is important to work on prevention and delay.[4] While we may no longer wish to be the life of the party as we enter our older years, social connection is important because it helps us to stay informed, be cared for, and show care towards others, test out our ideas and beliefs, and feel acknowledged as a worthwhile human being.

Other dementia risks include those that can be treated medically such as high blood pressure, high low-density lipid levels, and hearing impairment, pointing to the importance of maintaining contact with health professionals as we age. These modifiable risk factors are also implicated in other health conditions such as heart disease, as are lifestyle changes that can be made even in our 80s and 90s, for example reducing alcohol consumption (or giving it up altogether), managing weight, and keeping active.[5]

It's not only physical and cognitive issues you have to deal with – you may find people treat you differently too. Personally, we don't mind when a younger person gives up their seat for us on public transport – quite the opposite! But it can feel dehumanising if you're treated as if incompetent or unable to have input into decisions about your own care. How beneficial it is to be part of cultures, families, or residential groups in which the aged are honoured and admired; their dignity respected; and efforts made to balance needs for both independence and nurture.

The grief, sadness, and disorientation if a partner or dear friend dies is yet another burden that the elderly must often bear. Maintaining social connection in these situations takes psychological effort. Nevertheless, there are resources available to assist (see resource section), and it is important to be aware of these and take advantage of them if need be.

Now let's talk about the gains! Just as well, old age has some positive features. This can be a time of life to take stock, relax, cherish your loved ones, and consider your legacy. You've seen it all and survived; gratitude, satisfaction with a life well lived, contentment, and perhaps even wisdom can be the outcomes.

What makes for a happy old age? It has been argued that to some extent, it's a choice, given that both preparation and psychosocial work are needed, although of course there's also an element of luck.[6] Studies of life satisfaction in many countries (for example, UK, Germany, China, and Australia) show that life satisfaction in the second half of life peaks at around retirement age (55–75 years) but drops back as we move closer to death, between 80 and 90 years of age. But not all 'geriatrics' (as some studies label this group) are miserable! Happiness in these years, not surprisingly, is predicted by adequate finances, and both physical and mental health.[7] These in turn are predicted by modifiable factors such as conservative financial habits (e.g., saving, cautious investment) and a health-promoting lifestyle (e.g., dietary restraint, non-smoking, limited alcohol use, physical activity, good sleep patterns, cognitive challenges, social inclusion). These are all habits that tend to involve forethought and preparation, although several writers note that even when you're 80, it's not too late to work toward improvements that pay off in terms of feeling good.[8] Managing your health, social connection, a sense of engagement and purpose, and a positive outlook all contribute. More difficult to modify can be the health benefits or dangers of where you live, your opportunities and ability to achieve financial stability, and perhaps most important of all, your own temperament and attitudes.

A LIFESPAN DEVELOPMENTAL APPROACH

Psychologist Erik Erikson's eight stage theory of human development conceptualises the positive outcome of this final stage of psychosocial development as a feeling of wholeness and meaning that he names 'a sense of integrity'.[9] He describes this stage as 'a retrospective accounting of one's life to date; how much one embraces life as having been well lived, as opposed to regretting missed opportunities'.[10] In earlier chapters we discussed how at each stage of psychosocial development, Erikson theorises that we face a 'crisis' between a positive psychological state (such as a sense of identity, generativity, or integrity) and a negative, maladaptive psychological state. In the case of this eighth stage of development, the negative state is 'despair' – in which a person is prone to bitterness and regret, has trouble seeing meaning in life, ruminates over past mistakes, and is disposed toward depression. Although almost everyone has those negative feelings at some time or other, successful resolution of the integrity versus despair crisis tips the balance toward the positive characteristics, thus providing the foundation to psychological wellbeing in old age.

What factors aid in this psychosocial crisis resolution? A stable sense of ego integrity is more likely to eventuate among those who have strong family and friendship relationships, who feel pride in their work and life achievements, and who believe they have made worthwhile contributions to others, for example through their descendants, care and mentoring of others, and community involvement.[11] One important opportunity for the elderly is to be given the chance to reflect back on life, to reminisce, to tell their story.[12] This process can facilitate acceptance, not just of one's successes but also of mistakes and limitations. It can help bolster sense of accomplishment and engender feelings of peace and wisdom.

Positive thinking strategies to strengthen sense of integrity include practicing gratitude by focussing on one's life advantages and joys, reframing perceived failures as learning experiences, and letting go of long-held resentments toward others. Gratitude journalling – in which you reflect on and write down the things that you were grateful for each day – has become a popular practice among all age groups, as an aid to encouraging optimism and positive thinking. Further practical strategies include taking time to enjoy nature and the small pleasures of the moment, exploring your interests, learning new things, and maintaining curiosity about the world. Some will find comfort in religion and the spiritual aspects of existence.[13] What is particularly important is allowing yourself to ask for help from others if needed. Consider the idea that through asking friends, family, and care workers for help, you are providing them with the psychosocial benefits of practicing altruism!

WHEN WILL YOU BE OLD?

Old age might feel like something that hasn't happened to you yet. According to new research, as life expectancy increases, so too does our idea of how we decide who is old.[14] A German study of over 14,000 people aged between 40 and 85 years and surveyed longitudinally over 25 years, showed a relationship between one's current age and beliefs about when old age begins. For those aged about 64, the average perceived onset of old age was approximately 75 years. However, each further four to five years of actual ageing led to the perceived onset of old age increasing by about one year. Additionally, those who saw old age as coming earlier were more likely to be younger, male, and reported more loneliness, more chronic diseases, and poorer self-rated health. The conclusion drawn is that old age is 'deeply subjective' and whether you define yourself as old will depend on how you feel, your environment, and the attitudes of those around you.

We, the authors of this book, are both in our ninth decade and starting to feel old! But we are still working – not for a living but for the cognitive challenges and social interaction that this exercise provides. According to the US-based Pew Research Center, 9 per cent of Americans aged 75 and older are still working, although not necessarily full time.[15] The late Queen Elizabeth II worked until she died at age 97, no doubt due to her sense of duty but hopefully also because she found meaning and pleasure in her role. A recent report of a 101-year-old Ohio woman who, on most days, drives 20 minutes to her work in a fabric shop, quoted this doughty lady as saying that she had tried to retire on several occasions but found she missed the routine and the company of her co-workers.[16] At least in countries with adequate social welfare and pension systems, the majority of those still working past 80 do so because they enjoy it and still have the energy to engage.

As might seem obvious from the discussion previously, as well as chronological age (the number of years you have been alive), we can also talk about psychological age – the age we feel. Yet another assessment of ageing has been described as biological age, which is defined by how much your DNA has been altered by a chemical reaction called methylation.[17] It is, in a sense, a measure of how much damage your body has experienced, how 'worn out' you are, and it is influenced by genetic make-up, disease, lifestyle, and environmental factors. People age biologically at different rates, depending on these factors. Some new research suggests that biological ageing may be flexible, the authors concluding that while environmental, physical, and mental stressors can significantly age a person biologically, the body can under certain circumstances naturally reverse this effect, lowering the chance of early mortality.[18] Commenting on this research, Noa Leach notes that the study did not examine how recovery might proceed, although the study authors speculate that both physical and mental rest (relaxation) are important.[19] You can find out more about biological age and how it is measured in the chapter footnote.[20] The 'standing on one foot' method is particularly intriguing!

WHAT WILL YOU BE DOING WHEN YOU ARE 80 OR 90?

Jeremy Walston, director of the Human Aging project at Johns Hopkins University, has been quoted as saying this: 'If you take a room full of 80-year-olds, 15% are frail and vulnerable. Sixty percent have some health problems that are slowing them down. The rest are robust and active'.[21] This latter group will be the ones most likely to be working still in some capacity or fully engaged with their hobbies and social interactions, including sporting and cultural activities, volunteering, active grandparenting (or great-grandparenting), and other pursuits. The 60 per cent majority must manage their health problems but will clearly benefit by a positive approach to continue engagement in the world. The frail and vulnerable elderly will need care, and it is important that this care also enables the older person to feel safe, secure, loved, and valued. Making the best of old age, whichever group you fit into, will be greatly assisted by decisions and preparations made earlier in life – see our tips at the end of the chapter. One goal of the Human Aging Project is to develop a mid-life 'score' that assesses how individuals are ageing during their middle years and what they can do to prolong health and optimal functioning. Researchers have noted that to adequately develop this score as a meaningful diagnostic tool will require making decisions about how to combine genetic information with lifestyle, personality, environmental and other factors.

What are the characteristics of those who make it to 80 and beyond in good health? Swedish researchers Johansson and Thorvaldsson followed up a group of 699 identical and same-sex fraternal twin pairs from age 80 until death, to see if they could shed light on this question.[22] They gathered data on genetics, health, physical activity, lifestyle, personality, and demographics of their sample. Recognising that their study group were already 'hardy survivors', they were curious as to what factors improved survival rates among those who had reached old age in the chronological sense. Using sophisticated statistical analyses, they concluded that only about 12 per cent of the between-person variability in age of death (conditional on being alive at age 80) could be ascribed to genetic influences. Around one quarter of the variability was attributed to similar or shared environments, while the major source of differences between those who survived longer and those who didn't, in this group of already elderly individuals, related to factors specific to the individual. Some of these factors were modifiable, even in old age (for example, non-smokers and those with normal blood pressure lived longer). And even when disease status was controlled for, social and self-perception variables were significant predictors of living longer, including social embeddedness, self-evaluation of health, and life satisfaction. The authors concluded that longevity is improved not only by the avoidance of certain diseases, but by 'maintaining a useful and satisfying role in society, preserving good physical functioning, not smoking, and conserving a positive view of life'.[23] Attitude and a sense of purpose are important. In short, if you want to live to 100, you need a reason to get up in the morning.

TIPS: PREPARING FOR OLD AGE IN YOUR RETIREMENT (OR PRE-RETIREMENT) YEARS

Before you get (or feel) old, here are some reminders about things to do. If you're already over 80 and reading this, it's probably not too late!

PRACTICAL PREPARATIONS

1. Get your medical team together. Find a general practitioner whom you trust and can communicate with (and is not going to retire before you expire, if possible). Similarly, find out where you can access other key health professionals that you need or might need (e.g., optician, audiologist, physiotherapist, psychologist, dentist, etc). As a minimum, timetable in regular checks for your eyes, teeth, and hearing.

2. Make a will including what to do with items of importance to you but not of monetary value. Consider and discuss with family organising who will have power of attorney if you are unable to manage finances. Consider too an advanced care directive, which allows adults to document their preferences for future medical treatment if they are not in the position to make these decisions themselves (for example if in a coma).

3. Explore housing options for your older years, even if you're not planning to move at the moment. Some will prefer to 'age in place' in the family home, others to downsize to more manageable accommodation. Downsizing might simply involve moving somewhere smaller and more conveniently situated, with less garden or repairs to deal with, but there is also the possibility of retirement villages and aged care, depending on how much assistance you need. It's important to know what is available, practical, and financially accessible for you, as well as the pros and cons of these options before you commit to change.

4. Find out about support services. What do your state, local council, and community organisations have available for in-home support as your needs for assistance increase? Example might include meals on wheels, food banks, district nursing services, or help with household chores.

5. Keep up-to-date with communications. Upskill yourself on the computer and mobile phone so you can stay connected. Consider purchasing a smart watch that will automatically connect to appropriate help if you have a fall. Know how to dial emergency

and to quickly contact a support person if you need assistance with health or urgent household matters. Update yourself about online banking and how to avoid scams.

EMOTIONAL AND SOCIAL PREPARATIONS

6. Practice gratitude – think about the benefits that life has given you. Thank those who have helped, inspired, or made your life better in some way.

7. Focus on the positive – enjoyment of nature, beauty, relationships, and just taking pleasure in those small moments of happiness

8. Stay socially connected. Keep in touch with old friends and make some new ones in your locality. Community organisations often provide opportunities for social interactions such as book clubs, walking or seniors' exercise groups, sporting clubs, and other activity groups/classes.

9. Take classes in something that interests you. Learning new things is good for your mental health and flexibility, as well as for your social interactions. Attending classes (in person or online) can help structure your day and, more importantly, provides challenges that you can maintain in your older years.

10. Let go of grudges, enmities, and resentments. Apologise to those whom you have harmed.

11. Relax, reminisce, tell your story.

8

MAKING THE MOST OF RETIREMENT

So much to do, so little time, or so much time, so little to do? Which is it to be?

For some of us the onset of retirement can create anxiety because we don't know what to expect. What will life look like when work no longer consumes the majority of our waking hours, and how we will define ourselves when our job is no longer a key part of our identity? What should retirement look like, and how should we be spending our time?

Over three decades ago, Betty Frieden[1] coined the term 'human work' to describe the unique opportunities available in retirement. Human work refers to the tasks, however large or small, that we choose freely, and that we do out of love rather than obligation. As one writer puts it, 'Human work is a good term because it honours ageing – and retirement – in all its diversity and complexity'.[2] It also raises awareness of the many possibilities for psychological growth in ageing and old age.

As we have seen in previous chapters, how we develop in retirement is influenced by a complex set of factors, including our histories, our personalities, our feelings about ourselves, and our relationship

DOI: 10.4324/9781003611783-8

to work. Some retirees have worked at jobs in which they felt power-less in the face of institutional policies and practices over which they had no control. Those who have endured long hours at difficult jobs that took a physical and psychological toll might choose to spend retirement, at least in the early years, in peace and quiet. Retirement for them brings blessed relief from the stresses of work. On the other hand, those for whom work was challenging and growth enhanc-ing might choose to pursue connections with work in retirement, although in different degrees and intensities, or to seek activities which they may have had to defer such as new and stimulating lei-sure pastimes. So what is 'good' retirement for one is not necessarily 'good' retirement for another. And of course, retirement may mean different things to the next generations of retirees, for whom work patterns may be more and more centred on working from home and on flexible working hours, perhaps resulting in less connection to a fixed workplace. Not to mention the increasing presence of robots and AI taking over many work functions!

How can today's retirees make the most of retirement? In think-ing about this question we need to take note of the close relation-ship between ageing and retirement. While retirement ages may differ considerably, this stage of life, as we saw in the previous chapter, is inescapably bound up with the ageing process. Retirees must face the usual health problems associated with getting older, as well as the social, psychological, and economic consequences of this life stage.

In this final chapter we focus on how to spend retirement in ways that are satisfying and growth promoting. We also canvass some of the regrets that were expressed by retired women in our own study. These resonate with comments from the many retired men and women we have talked to and what we have noted from the literature.

WHAT CONTRIBUTES TO 'SUCCESSFUL' RETIREMENT?

Previous chapters have detailed the many facets of retirement that contribute to wellbeing and satisfaction during this stage of life. It is not our intention to rehearse these here; rather to focus on one other important part of the retired life, namely, the activities retirees engage in.

> I am so happy in retirement, far more than I expected. I feared boredom and loss of meaning, but it's been easy to find so many worthwhile activities that I've never been busier. As so many others say: 'How did I ever find time to fit in work?' – it's so true . . . I've been able to study for sheer pleasure and interest, and I've been able to travel. As someone said to me recently: 'You live the life we all aspire to'. What's not to love?

No longer regarded as the end of life, retirement can be considered as a next life stage in which activities delayed by full-time work can be pursued and new life choices made. It is an opportunity to engage at last in those pastimes that matter most to each individual. The most common retirement activities people plan to pursue include travel, engaging in hobbies of various sorts, gardening, sport, getting fit through exercise, reading and relaxing, home renovations, and volunteering. Does the reality match these plans?

Yes, it does, although there are gender differences. Women are less likely than men to be engaged in organised sport, monitor financial investments, work part-time, or stay engaged with their pre-retirement occupation through reading, interest groups, or meetings. Men volunteer less than women, and when they do join up as volunteers, it is more likely in a supervisory role than as an 'on the ground' helper. Overall, women's retirement activities tend to be more social than men's, for example spending time with friends and caring for others. In our study, the most common activities women reported were reading, watching TV, and listening to music while home-related activities were also usual. In another study, exercising and keeping fit were important for many women who described exercise classes as being an 'organising' element in their day, structured and scheduled, much like work had been.

There is considerable evidence that leisure activities make a positive contribution to retirement adjustment, life satisfaction, and wellbeing.³ Recognition of this comes in the many online and in print magazines, available to retirees and seniors, that urge readers to be active, with suggestions as to how this may be achieved. Our research showed that the more women engaged in activities, the more satisfied they were with retirement and with life in general. Satisfaction with retirement and with life was also predicted by many specific activities, especially travel, spending time with friends, 'get fit' activities, attendance at clubs, and engaging in hobbies. Not surprisingly perhaps, satisfaction was not predicted by domestic chores or caring for others.

One question of interest is whether retirees typically take on new activities or retain old ones. In fact, some activities may have to be abandoned because of loss of physical capacity or energy or changing life circumstances. In these cases, retirement may act as an opportunity to begin new pursuits. We know that after retirement there is both continuity (maintaining pre-retirement activities) and disengagement (letting go of pre-retirement activities), but there has been little evidence available about the development of new interests and skills post-retirement. One small study of men and women who were highly engaged in leisure activities prior to retirement found that women were more innovative than men in their retirement leisure pursuits, while men were more likely to continue with their lifelong activities. Women tended to add more leisure roles after retirement rather than eliminate them.⁴ The researchers concluded that for women, the impetus to add new leisure roles was not retirement itself but their liberation from some of the gender role responsibilities that had previously defined their lives. Why men and women do and do not acquire new skills in retirement is a topic ripe for further research. Are gender differences in activities the result of early socialisation and gender roles? Are there differences in the opportunities available for men and women?

WHAT ARE THE REGRETS?

We were interested to find that the participants in our study had a great deal to say about difficulties they faced in their transition to retirement. After many years of structured daily life at work, the lack of structure may lead to a feeling of aimlessness and a corresponding erosion of wellbeing. As one of retired women in our study said:

> Adjusting to retirement is a slow process; in the beginning I had difficulty filling in my days and did not feel I was contributing much as a person.

Difficulties can be exacerbated when a partner is involved, as we have seen in Chapter 5. Although partnered individuals are more satisfied in retirement than unpartnered ones, for some the feeling of living out of each other's pockets can become overwhelming. It can take time to adjust. Another common problem is that the goals and desires of one partner can be sidelined in order to accommodate those of the other partner, who may or may not be retired. A plan for what you can and want to achieve in retirement will help avoid these problems. Don't wait until you actually retire. If you have a partner, talk to him/her about mutual (and single) activities. Two women in our study expressed it this way when asked what they might have changed about retirement:

> It would have been valuable if my partner and I had had more of a discussion on what my retirement might mean for us both together and individually. At times it feels as if our arrows are not pointing in the same direction as he is younger than me and not yet psychologically ready to retire.

> [I would] consider my needs over those of my husband. He retired some 10 years before I did and has been eager to take off to do the 'grey nomad' thing for many years now. Because he waited, somewhat impatiently, for me to finish doing my thing, I now feel under pressure to grant him his wish to take off on a whim. This makes it nigh on impossible for me to commit to the volunteer work that I feel I can, and should/would like, to do. I still have a great need to feel productive and useful, which

now I do not have. It is a source of great conflict and unhappiness in our house.

Many retirees wish they had planned better for the free time that retirement brings; this was a strong focus among those we studied. While the benefits of retirement planning, especially financial planning, are well recognised, not all felt this way. One woman reminded us that there can be a downside to planning, that life does not always follow an anticipated path, and flexibility is important.

Sometimes life throws curveballs. No amount of planning can prepare a person for curveballs. The ability to remain flexible, resourceful and true to yourself is key to being able to survive them. Planning my retirement would not have helped me with regard to unexpected violence and trauma . . . the only thing that helped has been to have faith that good people will come into your life and support you through that transition as best as possible. The danger in 'planning' is it sets up 'expectations'.

Many comments referred to the benefit of a gradual move into retirement via part-time work where possible, thereby offering retirees the opportunity to decide what they wanted to achieve post-retirement and to plan accordingly.

I think working part time leading to retirement would have been advantageous. So would seeing what volunteer options were available and trying them out on non-working days. Having said that, working part time in my job wasn't an option.

The concept of flexible work is not new, and many companies offer it in some form – job sharing, working from home, compressed workweeks, and part-time schedules. But such programmes are usually small in scale and, in practise, are largely taken up by those with family commitments. And often employees who participate pay a penalty; they see their careers suffer for it or retire with less financial security, as we have seen in our earlier discussion of women's often fragmented working lives. If companies offer flexibility programmes that are easily accessible to older workers and structure these so that people who participate don't feel that they're being sidelined, there is a two-way benefit. The employer retains the skills and experience of older people, and the employee is able to move into full-time retirement at his or her own pace.

Regret at retiring early, either voluntarily or involuntarily, was not uncommon. We have noted the advantages and disadvantages of early retirement in earlier chapters, with financial outcomes being one of the most problematic. Similarly, for those whose retirement timing is determined by others, the opportunities for planning may be limited, and as we have seen, these retirees may find themselves less satisfied with retirement than those who retire at a time of their choosing.

Finally on planning, one woman told us:

> If there'd been a program you could do to really think through what retirement would mean – what I'd lose and what I'd gain – so I could be better prepared, I would have done that.

Interestingly, a search of the internet found a great concentration on pre-retirement financial planning programmes although, presumably, many of these would also provide information on other key aspects of retirement. Such a pre-retirement programme, from our perspective, would include information (and homework!) on our four 'pillars' of retirement life – finance/housing, health, social relationships, and identity/purpose. Earl[5] suggests businesses can help prepare their employees for retirement by providing access to pre-retirement planning and by thinking about retirement as part of a career development process, that encourages where possible a gradual move to part-time work if this is desired. The Australian Bureau of Statistics reports about 40 per cent of Australians want to work part time before permanently leaving the workforce, but their goal is not met by action. The main reasons for this are fear of what their employer will think if they ask for part-time work and the lack of readiness of employers to embrace the idea of staged retirement. Clearly, the most effective programmes are those that discuss further employment possibilities and, as well, cover our four pillars of retirement life.

PLAN FOR A POSITIVE RETIREMENT

So how do we ensure a smooth transition to retirement? We need to spend just as much time thinking about what we need and want from our retirement as we spend planning for it financially. While each person's needs will differ, there are some common ways in which good planning can help establish good retirement.

As discussed in Chapter 5, maintaining or establishing social connections is a key factor. For many people, the work environment is one important source of friends and social contacts. While retirement does not necessarily mean these connections are lost, it does require some effort in seeking out old and finding new friends whether through a part-time job, clubs, or any type of organised social activities. Staying active is another important element in healthy retirement, either through organised sports or activities, taking long walks, gardening, or having the grandchildren for the day. There are many 'get fit' groups that offer older people the opportunity to strengthen their bodies and stave off ill health. Getting out of your comfort zones and into a new environment can do you good as well as spark new interests. If you have a partner, try to plan retirement activities together; communicate openly about issues that may arise as you transition to retirement.

Creative pursuits also fulfil retirement social and intellectual needs for many retirees. Opportunities abound to try out new creative activities, or extend commitment in pre-existing hobbies, through the plethora of classes and interest groups now available to seniors, many of them free or low cost. One mental exercise that has been suggested for those who are not sure what would interest them is to reflect back on what you enjoyed as a child. Often it is these activities that will re-awaken enthusiasm in later life. Examples include painting, craft, model making, and creative writing.

Importantly, plan your retirement financial needs. How much do you think you will need after you stop paid work? At age 65 the average lifespan is 86; at age 85, the expectation is 92. 'The longer you live, the longer you are likely to live' with women living longer than men. The post-retirement lifespan has been conceptualised by some authors as having three health-related stages: disability-free years, years with some disability, and dependent years. Quite clearly, the cost of retirement during these stages will differ, and the last stage is going to be significantly more costly than the first two for most retirees. So careful planning is essential to ensure that you have adequate finances at this point in your life. But also consider how you spend your funds early in retirement in order to get the most out of this period of your life. Is drawing down on superannuation or other savings to fund travel or other life circumstances the best way to use your funds? Is downsizing into smaller or different accommodation the best option for you? These are the sorts of questions that we rarely address early in retirement, but the answers we choose may have great bearing on our later financial security.

BEING OPTIMISTIC

The discipline of positive psychology has examined the ways and means in which optimism and positive thinking influence health and happiness. Flowing from this approach there are new research centres for positive ageing springing up in universities with a remit to find solutions to some of the key challenges facing an ageing population, including mobility, isolation and loneliness, changing spousal relationships, workforce participation, and sexual health, among other issues. These centres are often focused on how society perceives and promotes positive ageing and wellbeing. Their aims are to change the negative perceptions we have of ageing and the competencies of the aged, and to encourage communities to develop supportive environments for healthier ageing.

Husband-and-wife authors Patricia Edgar and Don Edgar argue in *Peak, Reinventing Middle Age*[6] that middle age can be the apex of our lives, a time in which we capitalise on all we have experienced and learnt. They suggest that increased longevity means that all of us need to rethink our responsibility for looking after ourselves and contributing to society beyond our 50s and 60s. It's a very optimistic book, using recent research to explore opportunities and blockers to productive ageing. The mini biographies that form the second part of the book show that flexibility in the later years can be the key to embracing a satisfying lifestyle. Research into longevity shows clearly that those who age successfully have enjoyed fulfilling lives. They have used their later years well, continuing a 'purposeful' life and being resilient in times of hardship. As the authors note,

> [S]ome aspects of ageing well are negotiable. The sooner we pay attention to them the better the outcome. The successful middle-aged are generally self-motivated and community-minded, manage their routines and their needs independently, and, although lonely from time to time, most are not isolated. They are not consumed by regrets and have learned to live day by day, remaining interested and interesting. Throughout their lives they have felt loved and worthwhile.[7]

We know that wellbeing is tied to having meaning and purpose in life, to having a reason to get out of bed for every day. There are many ways to achieve this, and individuals will have different methods of doing so. Staying fit and healthy after retirement is one way to maintain the quality of our life. It is true that the less we do, the less we will be able to do. A key to staying healthy is to eat well. To do this, one needs to know and follow recommended dietary choices as we have seen in an earlier chapter. Having enough good quality sleep is fundamental for wellbeing. When we're tired, it makes these other factors, such as getting exercise, eating well, and finding meaning in life, much more difficult.

Importantly, research reveals that our attitude to life has a great impact on our emotions. We know that a positive attitude is correlated with happiness, health, and better relationships. For older people their attitude to ageing is significant. Viewing ageing as a negative process is correlated with poorer outcomes than those who view age more positively and focus more on what they can do rather than what they can't. This is particularly so when dealing with the inevitable illnesses, aches, and pains of old age.

And of course having strong connections with other people and the community is vital for maintaining a positive attitude to retirement, while loneliness and isolation are associated with poor outcomes. There is a need to actively protect oneself against isolation, and there are many ways to do that: keep in touch with old friends, join local clubs, volunteer for an organisation, start and continue hobbies, enrol in a new course, and so on. Retirement is a time when you can experiment with different activities. You have the time, and after a lifetime of experiences, your self-esteem is robust enough to deal with a few mistakes and the occasional failures.

Finally, our research with grandparents[8] showed us how important laughter and play are for wellbeing. Many told us that this was one of the best aspects of grandparenting – the ability (and willingness) to discover their inner child and to throw themselves into fun behaviour. This sense of playfulness was regarded by grandparents as one of the best features of their interactions with grandchildren. It is not hard to imagine that this positive attitude might be part of an adaptive approach to life more generally, for example, in keeping connected to younger generations and the very different lives they lead. Losing that sense of play can easily lead to a dull, humdrum existence that can be hard to overcome. Finding something to laugh at and someone to laugh with can be the best therapy of all.

In short, take the opportunity to reframe negative attitudes towards growing older and find ways to make the most of these new stages in life – retirement and ageing – in which we are calmer, wiser, and more able to see events through the perspective of time. An oft quoted comment about old age sums it up well:

> None of us are getting out of here alive, so please stop treating yourself like an afterthought. Eat the delicious food. Walk in the

sunshine. Jump in the ocean. Say the truth that you're carrying in your heart like hidden treasure. Be silly, be kind, be weird. There's no time for anything else.[9]

What will make you happy in your retirement? Do you love to socialise with friends? Do you love being with your grandchildren? Do you want to travel, perhaps become a 'grey nomad'? Do you want to commune with nature – in the garden or on long walks in the country? Do you want to spend this period of your life giving back to your community? There are many, many options for you to remain engaged, as busy as you want to be and fulfilled. You could also consider growing old disgracefully – doing things that may seem out of character, perhaps a bit 'naughty', not quite approved of by society. The choices you make will, of course, be determined by many factors, chief among these being your health and your financial state. But don't let these choices be determined by others or artificially limit your own sense of what is achievable. Take courage and use this precious time in ways that give you joy, purpose, and meaning.

RESOURCES

In most countries, organisations including national and state or county governments, local councils, religious groups, and charities provide information and support services for retirees and the elderly. To get you started, here is a selection of useful websites for those living in the UK, US, or Australia.

UK

AgeUK: This group offers information and support to UK seniors through its webpage, telephone helplines, shops, day centres, classes, social and exercise activities, financial advice, and a wide range of services. Many of these services are free or low cost. https://www.ageuk.org.uk/services/

GOV.UK: This site provides information on eligibility for (and how to access) pension and cost of living support for those aged 60 and over in the UK. https://www.gov.uk/cost-of-living/60-or-over. One section of this site is about planning retirement income and it includes a step-by-step guide: https://www.gov.uk/plan-retirement-income

NHS.UK: has a guide for individuals with care and support needs, their carers, and those planning for their future care needs. https://www.nhs.uk/conditions/social-care-and-support-guide/introduction-to-care-and-support/

Retirement Matters: This website includes information about purchasing retirement related products and services including those related to travel, finance, legal, health and lifestyle issues. www.retirement-matters.co.uk/

USA

US government retirement website: Information about retirement and pension benefits, along with retirement planning tools and further useful material is available on this site, for the assistance of US citizens. www.usa.gov/retirement

US Department of Health and Human Services: This website includes information on programs for older adults including those associated with housing, health, and long-term care. https://www.hhs.gov/programs/social-services/programs-for-seniors/index.html

US Aging: The aim of this organisation as stated in their website is to help 'older adults, people with disabilities and caregivers throughout the United States [to] live with optimal health, well-being, independence and dignity in their homes and communities'. The website lists links to a wide range of community services including those concerning health, well-being, social engagement, transportation, transitioning to care, etc. https://www.usaging.org/hcbs

AUSTRALIA

Aged Care: The various aged care services funded, part-funded or registered by the Australian government are listed and explained on this site. https://www.health.gov.au/topics/aged-care. A step-by-step guide to accessing these services can be found on the related site, MyAgedCare. https://www.myagedcare.gov.au/ Services include help around the house and other assistance to 'age in place', short-term care provisions (for example if you are recuperating from a medical procedure), and information about types of aged care facilities and how they are accessed.

National Seniors Australia: This not-for-profit organisation advocates for better outcomes for older Australians. They address issues including affordable housing, age discrimination, health costs, poverty, aged care, and retirement concerns. Their website includes useful seniors' news, information, and advice. https://nationalseniors.com.au

Your Life Choices: This free online magazine for the over-50s presents regular articles on news, health and lifestyle issues, as well as advice and guidance on legal, investment, and retirement concerns. Updates on changing laws and government resources for the over-50s are also a feature of the magazine. https://www.yourlifechoices.com.au/

NOTES

CHAPTER 1

1 Office for National Statistics (UK). (2016). *National life tables: 2013–2015*. Retrieved from 25 September 2024. www.ons.gov.uk/peoplepopulation andcommunity/birthsdeathsandmarriages/lifeexpectancies/bulletins/ nationallifetablesunitedkingdom/20132015.

2 Office for National Statistics (UK). (2024). *National life tables – life expectancy in the UK: 2020 to 2022*. Retrieved from 25 September 2024. https://www. ons.gov.uk/peoplepopulationandcommunity/birthsdeathsandmarriages/ lifeexpectancies/bulletins/nationallifetablesunitedkingdom/2020to2022.

3 Wikipedia. (2024, December 11). *Retirement age*.

4 Moore, S., & Rosenthal, D. (2018). *Women and retirement: Challenges of a new life stage*. London, UK: Taylor and Francis.

5 Rosenthal, D., & Moore, S. (2018). *The psychology of retirement*. 1st Edition. London, UK: Taylor and Francis.

6 Wang, M., & Shi, J. (2014). Psychological research on retirement. *Annual Review of Psychology, 65*, 209–233.

7 Weiss, R.S. (2005). *The experience of retirement*. New York, NY: Cornell University Press.

8 e.g., Hershey, D.A., & Henkens, K. (2013). Impact of different types of retirement transitions on perceived satisfaction with life. *The Gerontologist, 54*, 232–244.

9 Everingham, C., Warner-Smith, P., & Byles, J. (2007). Transforming retirement: Re-thinking models of retirement to accommodate the experiences of women. *Women's Studies International Forum*, 30, 512–522.

10 Schlossberg, N. (2004). *Retire smart, retire happy: Finding your true path in life.* Washington, DC: American Psychological Association.

11 Jahoda, M., Lazarsfeld, P., & Zeisel, H. (2002). *Marienthal: The sociography of an unemployed community.* Piscataway, NJ: Transaction Publishers.

12 Lagier, S. (2013). Retirement: A full-time job. *Blog Post.* Retrieved from 11 December 2024. http://retiredsyd.typepad.com/retirement_a_fulltime_job/2013/05/finding-a-new-identity-in-retirement.html.

CHAPTER 2

1 Cussen, M.P. (2017, March 16). Journey through the six stages of retirement. *Investopedia.* Retrieved from 11 December 2024. www.investopedia.com/articles/retirement/07/sixstages.asp.

2 Australian Retirement Trust. (2024). *Equip Super says Australians are delaying retirement.* Retrieved from 11 December 2024. https://www.superannuation.asn.au/may-2024-super-news/.

3 Kiso, H., & Hershey, D.A. (2017). Working adults' metacognitions regarding financial planning for retirement. *Work, Aging and Retirement*, 3, 77–88.

4 Atwood, C. (2020). *Succession planning basics.* 2nd Edition. Jacksonville, FL: American Society for Training & Development.

5 Mason, S.R., Dies, K.G., & Morgan, L. (2020). *The leaders within: Engagement, leadership development and succession planning.* Chicago, IL: Health Administrative Press.

6 van den Bogaard, L. (2017). Leaving quietly? A quantitative study of retirement rituals and how they affect life satisfaction. *Work, Aging and Retirement*, 3, 55–65.

7 Price, C.A., & Nesteruk, O. (2015). What to expect when you retire: By women for women. *Marriage & Family Review*, 51, 418–440.

8 Sohier, L., van Ootegem, L., & Verhofstadt, E. (2021). Well-being during transition from work to retirement. *Journal of Happiness Studies*, 22, 263–286.

9 Price, C.A., & Nesteruk, O. (2015). What to expect when you retire: By women for women. *Marriage & Family Review*, 51, 425.

10 Erikson, E.H. (1963). *Childhood and society.* New York, NY: Norton.

11 Fisher, G.G., Chaffee, D.S., & Sonnega, A. (2016). Retirement timing: A review and recommendations for future research. *Work, Aging and Retirement*, 2, 230–261.

12 e.g., Stokel-Walker, C. (2024, April 8). Retiring in your 60s is becoming an impossible goal. Is 75 the new 65? BBC. Retrieved from https://www.bbc.com/worklife/article/20240404-global-retirement-increase-65-to-75; Khan, R., & Dander, A. (2023, October 9). Retirement age trends around the globe. *Visual Capitalist*. Retrieved from 11 December 2024. https://www.weforum.org/agenda/2023/10/retirement-age-trends-around-globe/.

13 Sohier, L., van Ootegem, L., & Verhofstadt, E. (2021). Well-being during transition from work to retirement. *Journal of Happiness Studies*, 22, 263–286.

14 e.g., Warren, D.A. (2015). Retirement decisions of couples in Australia: The impact of spousal characteristics and preferences. *The Journal of the Economics of Ageing*, 6, 149–162.

15 Gustman, A.L., & Steinmeier, T.L. (2005). The social security early entitlement age in a structural model of retirement and wealth. *Journal of Public Economics*, 89, 441–463.

16 Lumsdaine, R.L., & Vermeer, S.J.C. (2015). Retirement timing of women and the role of care responsibilities for grandchildren. *Demography*, 52, 433–454.

CHAPTER 3

1 Quote from a participant in our research study. All other quotes are from our study participants unless noted otherwise.

2 e.g., Super News. (2024, May). *Equip Super says Australians are delaying retirement*. Retrieved from 14 December 2024. https://www.superannuation.asn.au/may-2024-super-news/.

Stokel-Walker, C. (2024, April). Retiring in your 60s is becoming an impossible goal. Is 75 the new 65? BBC. Retrieved from 14 December 2024. https://www.bbc.com/worklife/article/20240404-global-retirement-increase-65-to−75.

3 Association of Superannuation Funds of Australia (ASFA). (2023, July). *ASFA urges action to close the retirement savings gender gap*. Retrieved from 14 December 2024. https://www.superannuation.asn.au/media-release/release-12-july-2023/.

4 Australian Bureau of Statistics (ABS). (2024, May). *Retirement and retirement intentions, Australia*. Retrieved from 14 December 2024. https://www.abs.gov.au/statistics/labour/employment-and-unemployment/retirement-and-retirement-intentions-australia/latest-release#income-at-retirement.

5 Board of Governors of the Federal Reserve System (USA). (2023). *Survey of consumer finances*. Retrieved from 14 December 2024. https://www.federalreserve.gov/econres/scfindex.htm.

6 Express (UK). (2017). *Pension warning: Tens of thousands of people retiring this year have NO savings*. Retrieved from 14 December 2024. www.express.co.uk/news/uk/782041/pension-warning-retirement-savings-britain-money-crisis.

7 Office for National Statistics (UK). (2022, June). *Census 2021: Saving for retirement in Great Britain: April 2018 to March 2020*. Retrieved from 14 December 2024. https://www.ons.gov.uk/peoplepopulationandcommunity/personalandhouseholdfinances/incomeandwealth/bulletins/pensionwealthingreatbritain/april2018tomarch2020.

8 Rosenthal, D.A., & Moore, S.M. (2019). *The psychology of retirement*. 1st Edition. Abingdon, Oxon, UK: Routledge, p. 34.

9 Bouchrika, I. (2024). 31 female CEOs of the S&P 500 by industry in 2024. *Research.com*. Retrieved from 14 December 2024. https://research.com/careers/female-ceos-of-the-sp−500.

10 Trinca, H. (2024, September 17). Female CEO ranks taking a hit. *The Australian*, p. 15.

11 OECD. (2023). *Reporting gender pay gaps in OECD countries*. Retrieved from 14 December 2024. https://www.oecd.org/en/publications/reporting-gender-pay-gaps-in-oecd-countries_ea13aa68-en.html.

12 Innocenti, S., Clark, G.L., & McGill, S.W. (2024). Experience of financial challenges, retirement concerns, and planning evidence from representative samples of workers in 16 countries. *Journal of Pension Economics and Finance*, 23, 183–201.

13 Golladay, C. (2016, November 15). Schwab survey finds major differences in how male and female millennials view retirement. *Business Wire, USA*. Retrieved from 29 January 2025. www.businesswire.com/news/home/20161115005264/en/Schwab-Survey.

14 Lusardi, A., & Mitchell, O.S. (2011). Financial literacy and retirement planning in the United States. *Journal of Pension Economics and Finance*, 10, 509–525.

15 Global Financial Literary Excellence Center (GFLEC). (2017). *Women and financial literacy: OECD/INFE evidence, survey and policy responses report*. Washington, DC: Russia Financial Literacy and Education Trust Fund, George Washington University.

16 Bucher-Koenen, T., Lusardi, A., Alessie, R.J.M., & van Rooij, M.C.J. (2016, February). *How financially literate are women? An overview and new insights. Working paper* 2016–1. Global Financial Literary Excellence Center (GFLEC).

17 Angrisani, M., Barrera, S., Blanco, L.R., & Contreras, S. (2021). The racial/ethnic gap in financial literacy in the population and by income. *Contemporary Economic Policy*, 39(3), 524–536.

18 Australian Bureau of Statistics. (2024, March 20). *Personal fraud.* Retrieved from 29 January 2025. https://www.abs.gov.au/statistics/people/crime-and-justice/personal-fraud/latest-release.

19 Statista. (2024). *Share of internet users in the United Kingdom (UK) who are able to identify scam e-mails as of November 2023, by age group.* Retrieved from 29 January 2025. https://www.statista.com/statistics/1386124/internet-users-recognize-scam-e-mails-uk-by-age/.

20 OECD. (2022). *Pension policy notes and reviews.* Retrieved from 14 December 2024. www.oecd.org/pensions/policy-notes-and-reviews.htm.

CHAPTER 4

1 World Health Organisation (WHO). (2024, August 7). *The top 10 causes of death.* Retrieved from 29 January 2025. https://www.who.int/news-room/fact-sheets/detail/the-top-10-causes-of-death.

2 Hessel, P. (2016). Does retirement (really) lead to worse health among European men and women across all educational levels? *Social Science & Medicine, 151,* 19–26.

3 Xue, B., Head, J., & McMunn, A. (2020). The impact of retirement on cardiovascular disease and its risk factors: A systematic review of longitudinal studies. *The Gerontologist, 60*(5), e367–e377.

4 Szabo, A., Allen, J., Stephens, C., & Alpass, F. (2019). Is retirement associated with physical health benefits? A longitudinal investigation with older New Zealanders. *Age and Ageing, 48,* 267–272.

5 Yeung, D.Y., & Zhou, X. (2017). Planning for retirement: Longitudinal effect on retirement resources and post-retirement well-being. *Frontiers in Psychology, 8,* 1300. https://doi.org/10.3389/fpsyg.2017.01300.

6 Engel, L., & Mihalopoulis, C. (2024, August 26). The loneliness epidemic: A holistic view of its health and economic implications in older age. *Medical Journal of Australia.* Retrieved from 29 January 2025. https://www.mja.com.au/journal/2024/221/6/loneliness-epidemic-holistic-view-its-health-and-economic-implications-older-age?.

7 Holt-Lunstad, J., Smith, T.B., & Layton, J.B. (2010). Social relationships and mortality risk: A meta-analytic review. *PLoS Medicine, 7*(7), e1000316.

8 Zhu, R. (2016). Retirement and its consequences for women's health in Australia. *Social Science & Medicine, 163,* 117–125.

9 Helldán, A., Lallukka, T., Rahkonen, O., & Lahelma, E. (2012). Changes in healthy food habits after transition to old age retirement. *European Journal of Public Health, 22,* 582–586.

10 Prakash, K.C., Vertanen, M., Tormalehto, S., Myllyntausta, S., Pentti, J., Vahtera, J., & Stenholm, S. (2022). Changes in life satisfaction during the transition to retirement: Findings from the FIREA cohort study. *European Journal of Ageing*, 19(4), 1587–1599.

11 Odone, A., Gianfredi, V., Vigezzi, G.P., Amerio, A., Ardito, C., d'Errico, A., Stuckler, D., & Costa, G., on Behalf of the Italian Working Group on Retirement and Health. (2021). Does retirement trigger depressive symptoms? A systematic review and meta-analysis. *Epidemiology and Psychiatric Sciences*, 30, e77, 1–24.

12 Li, W., Ye, X., Zhu, D., & He, P. (2021). The longitudinal association between retirement and depression: A systematic review and meta-analysis. *American Journal of Epidemiology*, 190(10), 2220–2230.

13 Barbosa, L.M., Monteiro, L., & Murta, S.G. (2016). Retirement adjustment predictors: A systematic review. *Work, Aging and Retirement*, 2, 262–280.

14 Hansson, I., Henning, G., Buratti, S., Lindwall, M., Kivi, M., Johansson, B., & Berg, A.I. (2020). The role of personality in retirement adjustment: Longitudinal evidence for the effects on life satisfaction *Journal of Personality*, 88(4), 642–658.

15 Ortolá, R, Sotos-Prieto, M., García-Esquinas, E., Galán, I., & Rodríguez-Artalejo, F. (2024). Alcohol consumption patterns and mortality among older adults with health-related or socioeconomic risk factors. *JAMA Network Open*, 7(8), e2424495.

16 Australian Institute of Health and Welfare. (2024). *Older people's use of alcohol, tobacco, e-cigarettes and other drugs*. Retrieved from 29 January 2025. https://www.aihw.gov.au/reports/older-people/lder-people-alcohol-drugs.

17 Bamburger, P.A. (2015). Winding down and boozing up: The complex link between retirement and alcohol misuse. *Work, Aging and Retirement*, 1, 92–111.

18 Landreat, M.G., Cholet, J., Bronnec, M.G., Lalande, S., & Le Reste, J.Y. (2019). Determinants of gambling disorders in elderly people – A systematic review. *Frontiers in Psychiatry*, 10, 837. Retrieved from 29 January 2025. https://pmc.ncbi.nlm.nih.gov/articles/PMC6886010/.

CHAPTER 5

1 Tambourini, C.R. (2007). The never-married in old age: Projections and concerns for the near future. *Social Security Bulletin*, 67, 25–40.

2 Patulny, R. (2009). The golden years? Social isolation among retired men and women in Australia. *Family Matters*, 83, 39–47, Australian Institute of Family Studies.

3 Damman, M., & van Duijn, R. (2017). Intergenerational support in the transition from work to retirement. *Work, Aging and Retirement*, 3(1), 66–76.

4 Rosenthal, D.A., & Moore, S.M. (2012). *New age nanas: Being a grandmother in the 21st century.* Newport, NSW, Australia: Big Sky Publishing, pp. 79–80.

   Moore, S.M., & Rosenthal, D.A. (2016). *Grandparenting: Contemporary perspectives.* London: Taylor and Francis.

   Moore, S.M., & Rosenthal, D.A. (2024). Grandparents and non-custodial child care: Joys and difficulties. *International Journal of Birth and Parenting Education,* 11(2), 27–31.

5 Social Security Office of Retirement Policy (USA). (2014). *Population profiles. Marital status and poverty.* Retrieved from 29 January 2025. www.ssa.gov/retirementpolicy/fact-sheets/marital-status-poverty.html.

   Tamborini, C.R. (2007). The never-married in old age: Projections and concerns for the near future. *Social Security Bulletin, 67*(2), 25–40.

6 Kendig, H., Gong, C.H., Cannon, L., & Browning, C. (2017). Preferences and predictors of aging in place: Longitudinal evidence from Melbourne, Australia. *Journal of Housing for the Elderly, 31*(3), 259–271.

7 Engel, L., & Mihalopoulos, C. (2024). The loneliness epidemic: A holistic view of its health and economic implications in older age. *Medical Journal of Australia,* 221(6), 290–292.

8 Bolton, M. (2012). Loneliness – The state we're in: A report of evidence compiled for the campaign to end loneliness. *Age UK Oxfordshire.* Retrieved from 30 January 2025. https://www.campaigntoendloneliness.org/wp-content/uploads/Loneliness-The-State-Were-In.pdf.

9 Hawkley, L.C., Hughes, M.E., Waite, L.J., Masi, C.M., Thisted, R.A., & Cacioppo, J.T. (2008). From social structural factors to perceptions of relationship quality and loneliness: The Chicago health, aging, and social relations study. *The Journals of Gerontology Series B: Psychological Sciences and Social Sciences,* 63(6), S375–S384;

   Hawkley, L.C., & Cacioppo, J.T. (2007). Aging and loneliness. *Current Directions in Psychological Science, 16*(4), 187–191.

10 Holt-Lunstad, J., Smith, T.B., & Layton, J.B. (2010). Social relationships and mortality risk: A meta-analytic review. *PLoS Medicine, 7*(7), e1000316.

11 Steptoe, A., Shankar, A., Demakakos, P., & Wardle, J. (2013). Social isolation, loneliness, and all-cause mortality in older men and women. *Proceedings of the National Academy of Sciences of the United States of America (PNAS),* 110(15), 5797–5801.

   Yu, B., Steptoe, A., Chen, Y., & Jia, X. (2020). Social isolation rather than loneliness is associated with cognitive decline in older adults: The China health and retirement longitudinal study. *Psychological Medicine, 51*(14), 2414–2421.

Crowe, C.L., Domingue, B.W., Graf, G.H., Keyes, C.M., Kwon, D., & Belsky, D.W. (2021). Associations of loneliness and social isolation with health span and life span in the U.S. health and retirement study. *The Journals of Gerontology Series A: Biological Sciences and Medical Sciences*, 76(11), 1997–2006.

12 Steffens, N.K., Cruwys, T., Haslam, C., Jetten, J., & Haslam, S.A. (2016). Social group memberships in retirement are associated with reduced risk of premature death: Evidence from a longitudinal cohort study. *BMJ Open*, 6, e010164.

13 Steptoe, A., Shankar, A., Demakakos, P., & Wardle, J. (2013). Social isolation, loneliness, and all-cause mortality in older men and women. *Proceedings of the National Academy of Sciences of the United States of America (PNAS)*, 110(15), 5797–5801.

14 Greenfield, E.A., & Marks, N.F. (2004). Formal volunteering as a protective factor for older adults' psychological well being. *Journal of Gerontology: Social Sciences*, 59B, S258–S264.

15 Steptoe, A., Shankar, A., Demakakos, P., & Wardle, J. (2013). Social isolation, loneliness, and all-cause mortality in older men and women. *Proceedings of the National Academy of Sciences of the United States of America (PNAS)*, 110(15), 5797–5801.

16 Stanley, I.H., Conwell, Y., Bowen, C., & Van Orden, K.A. (2014). Pet ownership may attenuate loneliness among older adult primary care patients who live alone. *Aging and Mental Health*, 18, 394–399.

CHAPTER 6

1 Erikson, E.H. (1963). *Childhood and society*. New York, NY: Norton.

2 Moore, S.M., & Rosenthal, D.A. (2017). *Australian women in retirement survey. Final research report*. Unpublished Document Available from the Authors.

3 e.g., Haslam, C., Lam, B.C.P., Branscombe, N.R., Steffens, N.K., Haslam, S.A., Cruwys, T., Fong, P., & Ball, T.C. (2018). Adjusting to life in retirement: The protective role of new group memberships and identification as a retiree. *European Journal of Work and Organizational Psychology*, 27(6), 822–839.

Jolles, D., Lamarche, V.M., Rolison, J.J., & Juanchich, M. (2023). Who will I be when I retire? The role of organizational commitment, group memberships and retirement transition framing on older worker's anticipated identity change in retirement. *Current Psychology*, 42, 15727–15741.

4 Wang, M., & Shi, J. (2014). Psychological research on retirement. *Annual Review of Psychology*, 65, 209–233.

Reitzes, D.C., & Mutran, E.J. (2004). The transition to retirement: Stages and factors that influence retirement adjustment. *International Journal of Aging and Human Development*, 59, 63–84.

Reitzes, D.C., Mutran, E.J., & Fernandez, M.E. (1996). Preretirement influences on postretirement self-esteem. *Journal of Gerontology: Social Sciences*, 51B, S242–S249.

5 Reitzes, D.C., & Mutran, E.J. (2006). Lingering identities in retirement. *The Sociological Quarterly*, 47, 333–359.

6 Bordia, P., Read, S., & Bordia, S. (2020). Retiring: Role identity processes in retirement transition. *Journal of Organizational Behavior*, 41(5), 445–460.

7 Topa, G., & Alcover, C. (2015). Psychosocial factors in retirement intentions and adjustment: A multi-sample study. *Career Development International*, 20, 384–408.

8 Zaniboni, S., Sarchielli, G., & Fraccaroli, F. (2010). How are psychosocial factors related to retirement intentions? *International Journal of Manpower*, 31, 271–285.

9 Barnes, H., & Parry, J. (2004). Renegotiating identity and relationships: Men and women's adjustments to retirement. *Ageing and Society*, 24, 213–233.

10 Barnes, H., & Parry, J. (2004). Renegotiating identity and relationships: Men and women's adjustments to retirement. *Ageing and Society*, 24, 213–233.

11 Herron, A. (2017). *Male engineers extending working life: Issues in ongoing professional practice development*. PhD thesis, Faculty of Business and Law, Swinburne University of Technology, Australia. Retrieved from 30 January 2025. https://research bank.swinburne.edu.au/file/2df8798a-58c1–4c20-acf9-e38361ab2d24/1/Alison%20Herron%20Thesis.pdf.

12 Price, C.A. (2003). Professional women's retirement adjustment: The experience of reestablishing order. *Journal of Aging Studies*, 17, 341–355.

13 Price, C.A. (2003). Professional women's retirement adjustment: The experience of reestablishing order. *Journal of Aging Studies*, 17, 348.

14 Borrero, L., & Kruger, T.M. (2015). The nature and meaning of identity in retired professional women. *Journal of Women and Aging*, 27, 309–329.

15 Reitzes, D.C., & Mutran, E.J. (2006). Lingering identities in retirement. *The Sociological Quarterly*, 47, 354.

16 Teuscher, U. (2010). Change and persistence of personal identities after the transition to retirement. *International Journal of Aging and Human Development*, 70, 89–106.

17 Moore, S.M., & Rosenthal, D.A. (2017). *Australian women in retirement survey. Final research report*. Unpublished Document Available from the Authors.

CHAPTER 7

1 Frijters, P., & Beatton, T. (2012). The mystery of the U-shaped relationship between happiness and age. *Journal of Economic Behavior & Organization*, 82(2–3), 525–542.

2 World Health Organisation (WHO). (2024, October 1). *Ageing and Health Fact Sheet*. Retrieved from 1 February 2025. https://www.who.int/news-room/fact-sheets/detail/ageing-and-health.

3 Buchanan, T., & McCarthy, C. (2024, November 11). Dementia is the chronic condition of the 21st century. *Insight+, Issue 44*. Retrieved from 1 February 2025. https://insightplus.mja.com.au/2024/44/dementia-is-the-chronic-disease-of-the-21st-century/.

4 Alzheimer's Society. (2024, May 10). *How many people have dementia in the UK?* Retrieved from 1 February 2025. https://www.alzheimers.org.uk/blog/how-many-people-have-dementia-uk.

5 Buchanan, T., & McCarthy, C. (2024, November 11). Dementia is the chronic condition of the 21st century. *Insight+, Issue 44*. Retrieved from 1 February 2025. https://insightplus.mja.com.au/2024/44/dementia-is-the-chronic-disease-of-the-21st-century/.

6 Selig, M. (2024, December 13). How people stay hopeful and happy after age 80. *Psychology Today*. Retrieved from 1 February 2025. https://www.psychologytoday.com/au/blog/changepower/202412/do-older-people-stay-hopeful-and-happy-after-age−80.

   Selig, M. (2020). *Silver sparks: Thoughts on growing older, wiser, and happier*. St Louis, MO: Nevertheless Press.

7 e.g., Sun, Y. (2023). Happiness and mental health of older adults: Multiple mediation analysis. *Frontiers in Psychology*, 14, 1108678.

   Frijters, P., & Beatton, T. (2012). The mystery of the U-shaped relationship between happiness and age. *Journal of Economic Behavior & Organization*, 82(2–3), 525–542.

8 e.g., Selig, M. (2024, December 13). How people stay hopeful and happy after age 80. *Psychology Today*. Retrieved from 1 February 2025. https://www.psychologytoday.com/au/blog/changepower/202412/do-older-people-stay-hopeful-and-happy-after-age−80.

   Selig, M. (2023, June 29/2024, June 29). On turning 80 years old and planning to reach 100. *Psychology Today*. Retrieved from 1 February 2025. https://www.psychologytoday.com/au/blog/changepower/202406/on-turning-80-years-old-and-planning-to-reach−100.

9 Erikson, E., & Erikson, J. (2010). *The lifestyle completed (extended version): A review*. New York: W.W. Norton & Co.

10 Erikson, E., & Erikson, J. (2010). *The lifestyle completed (extended version): A review.* New York: W.W. Norton & Co., p. 20.

11 Cherry, K. (2009/2023, February 28). Integrity vs. despair in psychosocial development. *Verywell Mind.* Retrieved from 1 February 2025. https://www.verywellmind.com/integrity-versus-despair−2795738.

12 e.g., Harris, C.B., Van Bergen, P., Strutt, P.A., Picard, G.K., Harris, S.A., Brookman, R., & Nelson, K. (2022). Teaching elaborative reminiscing to support autobiographical memory and relationships in residential and community aged care services. *Brain Sciences, 12*(3), 374.

13 e.g., Chen, Y., Okereke, O.I., Kim, E.S., Tiemeier, H., Kubzansky, L.D., & VanderWeele, T.J. (2024). Gratitude and mortality among older US female nurses. *JAMA Psychiatry, 81*(10), 1030−1038.

 Chida,Y., Steptoe,A., & Powell, L. (2009). Religiosity/spirituality and mortality: A systematic quantitative review. *Psychotherapy and Psychosomatics, 78*(2), 81−90.

 Cherry, K. (2009/2023, February 28). Integrity vs. despair in psychosocial development. *Verywell Mind.* Retrieved from 1 February 2025. https://www.verywellmind.com/integrity-versus-despair−2795738.

14 Wettstein, M., Park, R., Kornadt, A.E., Wurm, S., Ram, N., & Gerstorf, D. (2024). Postponing old age: Evidence for historical change toward a later perceived onset of old age. *Psychology and Aging, 39*(5), 526−541.

15 Fry, R., & Braga, D. (2023, December 14). The growth of the older workforce. *Pew Research Center.* Retrieved from 1 February 2025. https://www.pewresearch.org/social-trends/2023/12/14/the-growth-of-the-older-workforce/.

16 Pawlowski, A. (2023, August 8). Woman, 101, who still works and drives has simple tips for long life. *Today.* Retrieved from 1 February 2025. https://www.today.com/health/womens-health/101-year-old-woman-still-works-rcna98138.

17 Poganik, J.R., Zhang, B., Baht, G.S., Tyshkovskiy, A., Deik, A., Kerepesi, C., Yim, S.H., Lu, A.T., Haghani, A., Gong, T., Hedman, A.M., Andolf, E., Pershagen, G., Almqvist, C., Clish, C.B., Horvath, S., White, J.P., & Gladyshev, V.N. (2023, May). Biological age is increased by stress and restored upon recovery. *Cell Metabolism, 35*(5), 807−820.

18 Poganik, J.R., Zhang, B., Baht, G.S., Tyshkovskiy, A., Deik, A., Kerepesi, C., Yim, S.H., Lu, A.T., Haghani, A., Gong, T., Hedman, A.M., Andolf, E., Pershagen, G., Almqvist, C., Clish, C.B., Horvath, S., White, J.P., & Gladyshev, V.N. (2023, May). Biological age is increased by stress and restored upon recovery. *Cell Metabolism, 35*(5), 807−820.

19 Leach, N. (2023, April 24). Here's how you can reverse your biological age, according to breakthrough new study. *BBC Science Focus Magazine.* Retrieved from 1 February 2025. https://www.sciencefocus.com/news/reverse-ageing-caused-by-stress.

20 Steele, A. (2025, January 18). 5 simple ways to instantly find your 'biological age. *BBC Science Focus Magazine*. Retrieved from 1 February 2025. https://www.sciencefocus.com/the-human-body/find-your-biological-age.

21 Nitkin, K. (2023, March–April). Why do some 80-year-olds seem like they're 60? (And some 60-year-olds seem closer to 80?). *Dome*. Retrieved from 1 February 2025. https://www.hopkinsmedicine.org/news/articles/2023/03/why-do-some-80-year-olds-seem-like-theyre-60-and-some-60-year-olds-seem-closer-to-80-the-johns-hopkins-human-aging-project-looks-for-answers.

22 Johansson, B., & Thorvaldsson, V. (2021). What matters and what matters most for survival after age 80? A multidisciplinary exploration based on twin data. *Frontiers in Psychology*, 12, 723027.

23 Johansson, B., & Thorvaldsson, V. (2021). What matters and what matters most for survival after age 80? A multidisciplinary exploration based on twin data. *Frontiers in Psychology*, 13.

CHAPTER 8

1 Friedan, B. (1993). *The fountain of age*. New York, NY: Simon and Schuster.

2 Karpen, R.R. (2017). Reflections on women's retirement. *Gerontologist*, 57, 103–109.

3 Earl, J.K., Gerrans, P., & Halim, V.A. (2015). Active and adjusted: Investigating the contribution of leisure, health and psychosocial factors to retirement adjustment. *Leisure Sciences*, 37, 354–372.

4 Jaumont-Pascual, N., Monteagudo, M.J., Kleiber, D.A., & Cuenca, J. (2016). Gender differences in meaningful leisure following major later life events. *Journal of Leisure Research*, 48, 83–103.

5 Earl, J.K., & Archibald, H. (2014). Retirement planning and resources. *European Journal of Management*, 14(2), 21–36.

6 Edgar, P., & Edgar, D. (2017). *Peak: Reinventing middle age*. Melbourne, Australia: Text Publishing Co.

7 Edgar, P., & Edgar, D. (2017). *Peak: Reinventing middle age*. Melbourne, Australia: Text Publishing Co., p. 92.

8 Rosenthal, D.A., & Moore, S.M. (2012). *New age nanas: Being a grandmother in the 21st century*. Newport, NSW, Australia: Big Sky Publishing, pp. 79–80.

9 It is unclear as to the original source of this quote. Various options are referenced online, e.g., Anthony Bourdain (celebrity chef), Keanu Reeves, (actor), Anthony Hopkins (actor), Nanea Hoffman (influencer).

For Product Safety Concerns and Information please contact our EU
representative GPSR@taylorandfrancis.com
Taylor & Francis Verlag GmbH, Kaufingerstraße 24, 80331 München, Germany